EXPLORING THE LIFE, MYTH, AND ART OF ANCIENT GREECE

CIVILIZATIONS OF THE WORLD

EXPLORING

THE LIFE, MYTH, AND ART OF

ANCIENT GREECE

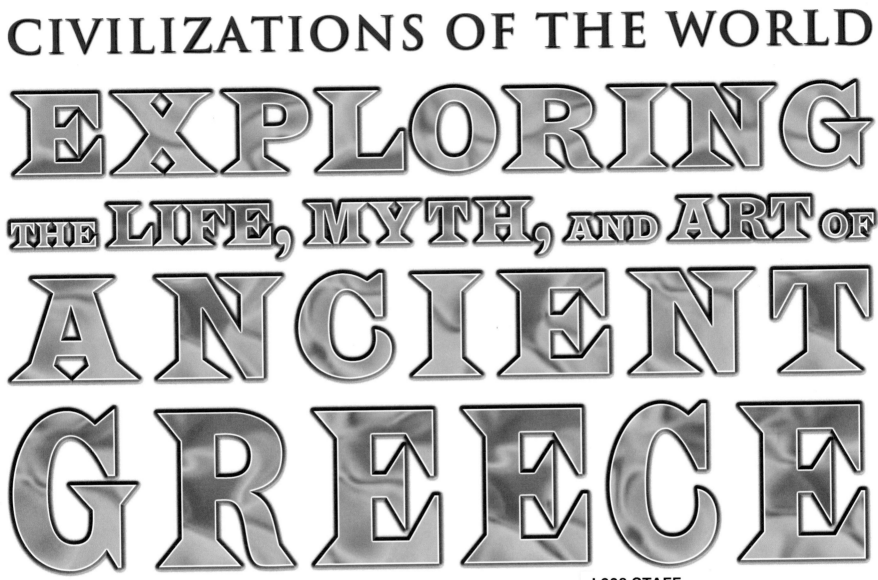

EMMA J. STAFFORD

ROSEN
PUBLISHING®

New York

This edition published in 2012 by:

The Rosen Publishing Group, Inc.
29 East 21st Street
New York, NY 10010

Additional end matter copyright © 2012 by The Rosen Publishing Group, Inc.

Library of Congress Cataloging-in-Publication Data

Stafford, Emma.
Exploring the life, myth, and art of ancient Greece/Emma J. Stafford.
    p. cm.—(Civilizations of the world)
Includes bibliographical references and index.
ISBN 978-1-4488-4830-0 (library binding)
1. Greece—Civilization—To 146 B.C.—Juvenile literature. I. Title. II. Series.
DF77.S59 2012
938—dc22

                                                                            2011009898

Manufactured in the United States of America

CPSIA Compliance Information: Batch #S11YA: For further information, contact Rosen Publishing, New York, New York, at 1-800-237-9932.

NOTES
Greek names (of places and people) have been transliterated to follow the Greek spelling rather than the Latinized spelling that may be more familiar to some readers, although a few traditional Latinized spellings have been retained where the correct Greek form might lead to confusion: for example, Oedipus instead of Oidipous; and Circe rather than Kirke. Any quotations from ancient Greek texts are the author's own translations.

CONTENTS

IMAGE AND IMAGINATION

The topography of Greece is dominated by two elements that had a profound effect on the development of ancient Greek civilization: mountains and the sea. On the one hand, these physical boundaries divided Greece into hundreds of autonomous city-states, each free to develop its own form of government. On the other hand, the presence of the sea made the Hellenes great travelers and traders, who exchanged ideas and goods with peoples all around the Mediterranean—stories from the Near East and Egypt informed the early development of Greek myth, which found expression at first in epic poetry and later in drama and all kinds of representational art. The land of Greece itself was the source of the marble and clay from which were fashioned the temples, sculpture, and painted pottery that provide our dominant images of Greek culture.

THE SOUL OF THE GREEKS

Each city-state had its own rituals for worshiping a particular selection of gods. However, some common features show that certain principles were fundamental to religious belief all over Greece—it was a polytheistic system, which included the major Olympian gods and goddesses, a host of minor deities such as nymphs and river gods, and an ill-defined group of semidivine heroes and heroines. Unlike the gods of many other ancient civilizations, those of the Greeks were almost all conceived of as being wholly human in form, with just a few exceptions, such as the goat-legged Pan. This tendency toward anthropomorphism can also be seen in the many human figures that personify such abstract ideas as Victory and Peace—it reflects a very human-centered view of the world.

There was no universally accepted religious text or creed. The occasional introduction to a particular city of a "new god"—either a deity imported from another region or an ideal newly elevated to divine status—suggests that there was flexibility in the system and some openness to new ideas. However, the fact that religion was basically conservative is revealed by the lack of change in many elements of ritual from Homer's time (eighth century BCE) until paganism's demise after Christianity became the official religion of the Roman Empire (312 CE).

In both Greek ritual and belief there was a strong emphasis on the here-and-now rather than the afterlife, and on reciprocity. The most common prayers that

LEFT: **This Attic black-figure cup was made ca. 570 BCE, not long after the hero Herakles was promoted to divine status in many areas of Greece. Here Herakles is being led by Athene and Hermes before Zeus and Hera on Olympos; the female figure standing between their thrones may be Hebe, "Youth" personified, who will be Herakles' divine consort.**

RIGHT: The diminutive temple of Athene Nike, celebrating Athene in her aspect as "Victory," perches on the bastion above the entrance to the Athenian Akropolis. Built in the late 420s BCE, elements of the Ionic architectural order can be seen in its slim, volute-topped columns and continuous frieze decorated with relief sculpture.

were recorded are for success in battle, abundance of crops, and the birth of healthy children, in return for which the would-be recipient would usually remind the deity of previous offerings made and promise more for the future. One divinity or another presided over every facet of human life, be it agriculture, hospitality, drinking, love, or sleep—even activities that might now seem far removed from the religious sphere, such as drama and athletics, developed as part of the worship of the gods. In daily life the Greeks were surrounded by images of the gods that were painted, carved in stone, or cast in precious metal; they not only stood as individual statues, but were used to decorate everything from temples and public buildings to crockery, jewelry, and clothes.

The few depictions we have of the afterlife reflect a general absence from Greek thought of any opposition between good and evil, since there was no clear correlation between good behavior or religious observance now and subsequent reward. Some mystery cults offered a privileged existence in the Underworld, and a few philosophers believed in the transmigration of souls, but generally people do not seem to have had strong expectations of life after death one way or the other: provided their bodily remains had received due burial, it was believed their soul would progress to a shadowy eternal existence in the Underworld (see pages 60–61).

KNOSSOS

The Minoan civilization flourished in Bronze Age Crete from ca. 2800 to 1450 BCE. From about 2000 BCE there developed a system of political, economic, and social organization centered on a number of palaces, such as Knossos, Phaistos, Mallia, and Zakros, in which each controlled the surrounding region. In ca. 1450 BCE all the palaces were destroyed—either by natural disasters, Mycenaean invaders from mainland Greece, or internal political disturbances— with the exception of Knossos, which survived for another 75 or so years under Mycenaean occupation, until it was destroyed in its turn.

The Knossos site was excavated between 1900 and 1932 by Briton Sir Arthur Evans, who published his finds in the lavish, multi-volume *Palace of Minos*. His work provided the foundations for the study of a culture that had previously only been known through the myths of King Minos, who was said by ancient writers to have ruled a great maritime empire. Many scholars today question Evans' romantic linking of Knossos with the legendary Minos, but there is no doubt that the world the archaeologist uncovered was a rich and sophisticated one. Three thousand clay tablets inscribed in Linear B (see page 46) found by Evans were eventually identified as inventories and accounts, indicative of a complex palace bureaucracy in Knossos' later years. The site today is still dominated by Evans' highly controversial reconstructions, which are more conjectural the higher above ground you go. The Grand Staircase, pictured here, gave access to various levels of the elaborately decorated Royal Apartments on the east side of the central courtyard; a few original steps are preserved, but the design of the pillars is reliant on ancient paintings and modern guesswork. Similarly interpretive are the frescoes now on display in Iraklion Museum, and doubts have been raised about the authenticity of the Boston "Snake Goddess" and other ivory figurines.

THE STORY OF THE GREEKS

The great sweep of Greek history—from the origins of Greek civilization through the "Dark Age" to the archaic, classical, and Hellenistic periods—begins with the earliest phase of Minoan civilization on the island of Crete (see page 11). On the mainland, the earliest people to leave us with traces of a highly structured society are the Mycenaeans, who began to arrive in Greece toward the end of the third millennium BCE. From around 1600 BCE they developed an advanced palace culture along similar lines to that of the Minoans. Excavations at Mycenae itself (see page 16), Tiryns, Pylos, and other palace sites have all unearthed clay tablets inscribed in so-called Linear B, which transcribes an early form of the Greek language. Between ca. 1200 and 1100 BCE, for reasons that are still unclear, the Mycenaean palaces appear to have suffered violent initial destruction followed by a period of decline and eventual abandonment. After this collapse of the Mycenaean world, the use of writing disappeared, along with wall-painting and other fine arts, because of which the ensuing three centuries are traditionally known as the "Dark Ages."

The dawn of the archaic period is traditionally marked by the foundation of the Olympic Games in 776 BCE. The art of writing was reintroduced around 750 BCE, using an alphabet borrowed from the Phoenicians. By the end of the eighth century BCE the *polis* ("city-state") had emerged as the principal form of social organization, constituted by an urban center and the surrounding rural territory (see pages 26–9). The appearance of the *polis* was closely tied to the emergence of the hoplite phalanx, a highly efficient fighting unit that required disciplined teamwork. In some states the phalanx provided a power-base for ambitious individuals who sought

LEFT: While the Minoan civilization was taking root in Crete, a contemporary culture was flourishing in the Aegean Cyclades ca. 3200–2000 BCE. Cycladic civilization is especially well known for the marble figurines found in its rich tombs. The figurines represent violin-shaped females with crossed arms or seated males playing musical instruments, such as this harp-player of ca. 2500 BCE.

RIGHT: The main map shows the important regions, city-states, and places of worship in the Hellenic world, while the smaller map (inset) of the Mediterranean has shaded areas to highlight the major spheres of Greek colonization, notably south Italy, Sicily, and around the coast of the Black Sea.

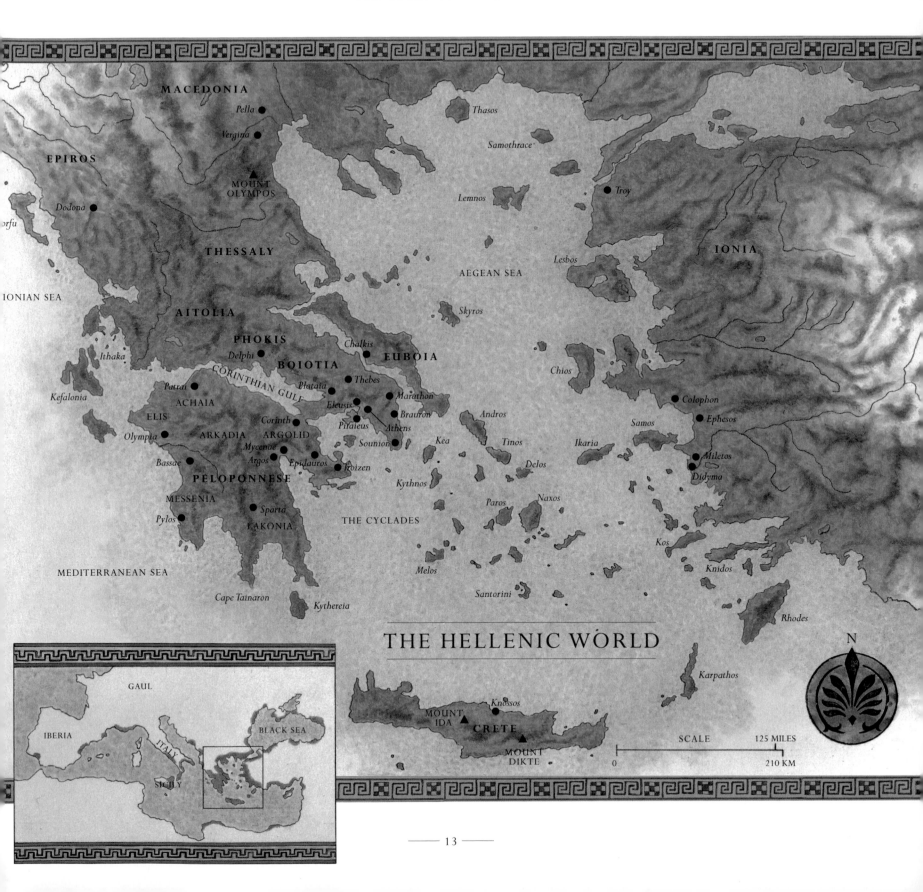

MACEDONIA

Pella ●

Vergina ●

EPIROS

▲ MOUNT OLYMPOS

Dodona ●

THESSALY

Thasos

Samothrace

Lemnos

Troy ●

IONIA

Corfu

IONIAN SEA

AITOLIA

AEGEAN SEA

Lesbos

PHOKIS

Skyros

Chalkis

Delphi

BOIOTIA

EUBOIA

Ithaka

Plataia

Thebes ●

Marathon ●

Chios

Patrai ●

CORINTHIAN GULF

Eleusis

Braῦron ●

Colophon ●

ACHAIA

Corinth ●

Piraieus

Andros

Samos

Ephesos ●

ELIS

Athens

Kefalonia

Olympia ●

ARKADIA

ARGOLID

Sounion ●

Kea

Tinos

Ikaria

Mycenae ●

Miletos ●

Bassae ●

Argos ●

Epidauros ●

Troizen ●

Kythnos

Delos

Didyma ●

PELOPONNESE

Paros

Naxos

MESSENIA

THE CYCLADES

Kos

Sparta ●

Pylos ●

LAKONIA

Knidos

MEDITERRANEAN SEA

Melos

Cape Tainaron

Kythereia

Santorini

Rhodes

THE HELLENIC WORLD

Karpathos

N

GAUL

BLACK SEA

Knossos ●

IBERIA

ITALY

MOUNT IDA ▲

CRETE

SCALE   125 MILES

SICILY

MOUNT DIKTE ▲

0   210 KM

sole rule, thereby helping to create the tyrants who are characteristic of the period. It was this era's political struggles, together with land-hunger, that may have prompted the establishment of Greek colonies all around the Mediterranean's shores (see inset, page 13).

The archaic period ended with the Persian Wars of 490–479 BCE, which were fundamental in shaping relations between the leading city-state powers of Athens and Sparta. It took the combined efforts of these two and a number of other Greek states to achieve final victory over Persia at Plataia (479 BCE) and usher in the classical age. Over the following fifty years Athens gained preeminence, until the Peloponnesian War of 431–404 BCE, at the end of which Sparta emerged as the foremost power of Greece. Sparta's hegemony was effectively ended by the disastrous defeat by Thebes at Leuktra in 371 BCE. Subsequent small-scale struggles left the southern Greek states open to the rising power of Macedon under King Philip II (359–336 BCE), who defeated an alliance of Athenians and Thebans at Chaironeia in 338 BCE.

Despite being an era of almost continuous warfare, the classical period saw all the cultural developments most associated with Greece's legacy to Western civilization. The tragedies of Aeschylus, Sophocles, and Euripides played on the Athenian stage; Herodotus, Thucydides, and Xenophon wrote their histories; Socrates expounded his philosophy, followed by Plato and later Aristotle; Demosthenes and Aeschines won fame as masters of rhetoric.

Once the whole of Greece was under Macedonian control, King Philip II's son, Alexander the Great (336–323 BCE), invaded Persia. His campaigns carried Greek culture to Egypt, Afghanistan, India, and the Persian Gulf. After Alexander's early

LEFT: The importance of seafaring in the Greek world is reflected in many representations of ships in vase-painting. This Attic black-figure cup, produced ca. 520 BCE and signed by the potter Nikosthenes (to the top right of the image), depicts two triremes in full sail, their battering rams clearly visible at the bow and steering oars at the stern.

death, his vast empire fragmented, with several of his former generals vying for power. The Hellenistic period begins with the three victorious "Successors" each establishing a ruling dynasty: the Ptolemies in Egypt, the Seleucids in Asia, and the Antigonids in Macedonia itself. The Antigonids' intermittent control over the whole of mainland Greece was challenged by the rise of various confederacies, of which the most successful was the Achaean League. From the late third century BCE the "clouds gathering in the west," as the historian Polybius dubbed the rise of Roman power, began to impinge on the eastern Mediterranean. A defining moment came in 146 BCE when the Achaean League was smashed and the prosperous Greek city of Corinth was laid waste by the Romans. From then on Greece was administered as the Roman province of Macedonia, with the Peloponnese and southern mainland becoming the separate province of Achaia in 46 BCE.

BELOW: The 1st-century BCE "Alexander Mosaic" from the House of the Faun at Pompeii is thought to be a copy of a late 4th-century BCE Greek painting. It shows a battle, sometimes identified as the Battle of Issos, between Alexander the Great and the Persian king Darius III. In this detail, the young Alexander, without helmet, boldly charges in to the attack.

MYCENAE

The entrance to the citadel at the center of Mycenae's palace complex is marked by the majestic Lion Gate. Built in the mid-thirteenth century BCE, the gate and walls surrounding it survived the mysterious destruction of ca. 1200 BCE to remain standing throughout antiquity—later Greeks thought that the massive stone blocks of the walls could only have been moved by giants such as the Cyclopes, at the behest of Mycenae's mythical founder Perseus. The Mycenae of myth subsequently passed into the hands of Atreus and his descendants, so becoming the site of the many bloody and incestuous deeds associated with the family.

It was these myths, especially as related by Homer, that inspired Heinrich Schliemann to excavate the site at Mycenae from 1874, after the success of his initial excavations of Troy in the early 1870s. When he uncovered the rich shaft graves within the akropolis, and their several gold death-masks, it was all too easy to associate them with the imagined splendors of the mythological past and heroes such as Agamemnon. Such romantic identifications should not be taken too seriously, but to this day the more spectacular of the *tholos* (or "beehive") graves outside the walls are popularly known by the names of members of the Atreid family, as the tombs of Klytaimnestra, Aegisthus, and Orestes. The "tomb of Agamemnon" was plundered in antiquity, but an idea of its wealth is conveyed by the ancient belief—recorded by the second-century CE Greek traveler Pausanias—that the structure had been the "treasury of Atreus."

THE ART OF THE GREEKS

After the collapse of Mycenaean culture (ca. 1200–1100 BCE), art continued to be produced but on a much more modest scale than hitherto. Throughout the "Dark Ages," pottery was decorated with simple patterns, which developed into the more complex geometric style after ca. 900 BCE (see pages 22–3). At the same time, small-scale sculpture of humans and animals flourished in the form of bronze and clay statuettes, which were dedicated to the gods at sanctuaries or buried with the dead as grave goods.

Large-scale figures of carved marble first appeared toward the end of the seventh century BCE. Initially these showed the influence of Egyptian proto-types, but a distinctively Greek style soon emerged. This style included the archaic male figure conventionally known as the *kouros* ("youth"), who is always nude and stands with his hands by his sides, one leg slightly advanced; the archaic female figure, the *kore* ("maiden"), is always fully dressed. Both male and female figures were erected in sanctuaries, where they represented either ideal wor-shipers or the deity him- or herself, and as grave markers to commemorate the dead. Advanced casting techniques were developed in the late sixth century, from which time bronze became the favored medium. Sadly, few original Greek bronzes have survived, and for the work of the most famous classical sculptors we are dependent on Roman copies (often in marble) and the observations of ancient writers. In the fifth century BCE the sculptor Pheidias was celebrated for his images of the gods, especially the massive chryselephantine (gold and ivory) statues of Athene Parthenos and Olympian Zeus, while his contemporary Polykleitos was better known for his portrayals of mortals. In the fourth century, Praxiteles popularized the female nude with his Aphrodite of Knidos, and Lysippos

LEFT: **This bronze head of the mythical griffin (see page 105) dates to ca. 650 BCE and would once have been attached, along with several others, to a tripod-cauldron. The griffin's reputation for watchfulness made it an especially suitable guardian for such valuable vessels.**

RIGHT: The "Auxerre *kore*,"
from Crete, is a limestone
statuette made ca. 640 BCE
and now named after the
town in France where she
was first exhibited. Her
small size (she stands just
25 inches, or 65 cm, high),
stiff frontal pose, flatness,
and wig-like hair are
typical of the "Daedalic"
style of mid-7th-century
BCE sculpture, a precursor
to the more rounded,
life-size forms of the
6th century BCE.

created the archetypal ruler portrait with his representations of Alexander the Great. Sculpture of the
Hellenistic period (323–31 BCE) took realism to new
extremes in the representation of individuals real or
imaginary, and dramatic group compositions such as
the Laokoon (see illustration, page 106) were created.

Stone temples also first appeared in the seventh
century BCE, and the idea of adorning them with
mythological scenes can already be seen in the painted
clay metopes (decorated panels) of the temple of
Apollo at Thermon (ca. 640 BCE). Later buildings
would be decorated entirely with relief sculpture,
which almost always represented scenes from myth.
Sometimes these reliefs would have a particular association with the location, but a number of themes are
found time and again throughout the Greek world:
gods fighting giants, Greek warriors fighting Amazons
or Centaurs, and the exploits of Herakles. Other relief
sculpture was carved on free-standing *stelai* as popular
offerings to the gods (known as votive reliefs) or they
bore inscriptions that recorded state decisions (decree
reliefs). Most common of all are funerary reliefs,
which replaced the earlier forms of grave marker
toward the end of the sixth century BCE; in the classical period these reliefs usually depicted the deceased
accompanied by family members.

Large-scale painting, on walls and wooden panels,
was also an important feature of Greek public art, but

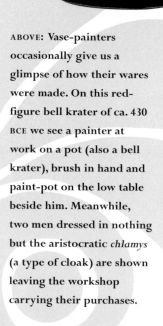

ABOVE: Vase-painters occasionally give us a glimpse of how their wares were made. On this red-figure bell krater of ca. 430 BCE we see a painter at work on a pot (also a bell krater), brush in hand and paint-pot on the low table beside him. Meanwhile, two men dressed in nothing but the aristocratic *chlamys* (a type of cloak) are shown leaving the workshop carrying their purchases.

what little we know of it has had to be pieced together from analysis of the few surviving examples preserved in tombs, comparison with contemporary vase-painting, of which many originals exist, and Roman copies. Ancient writers' anecdotes about fourth-century painters reveal that realism and *trompe l'oeil* effects were much admired; the most renowned practitioner of all was Apelles, court painter to Alexander the Great. We know that around 300 BCE floors were being decorated with figure scenes made out of pebble mosaics because of the examples that survive from the then Macedonian capital Pella—those mosaics were predecessors of the colorful tesselated mosaics of the Hellenistic and Roman periods.

Its relatively high survival rate means that pottery decorated with figure scenes is now by far the best represented category of Greek art, although its actual status and value in the ancient world is much debated. Such decorated pottery was clearly a step up from the plain ware used by the poorer classes, and less expensive than the gold- and silverware used by the most wealthy, but just how widely it was used is unknown. What is undisputed is the fact that painted vases are the most abundant source of images of Greek myth and daily life. From ca. 700 BCE it became common to decorate pots with mythological scenes, many of which can be firmly identified because of the practice of naming figures with inscriptions. Throughout the seventh century the main center for the production and export of painted pottery was Corinth—its wares easily recognizable by the paleness of the clay background and the rosette motifs used as decoration. From ca. 600 BCE the market was dominated by pottery from Attica painted in the black-figure technique, in which the deep-red clay provides a strongly contrasting background to figures painted in black slip, with incised details and occasionally some added white or purplish-red paint. Around 530 BCE the red-figure technique was invented, in which the figures are reserved in the red of the clay against a black background; details here are painted rather than incised, allowing for more subtle effects. Black-figure more or less died out after about 500 BCE, but red-figure continued to be used, its imagery moving away from the stylization of the archaic period to become ever more naturalistic. Around 400 BCE there was a marked decline in Attic production, and throughout the fourth century the red-figure pottery of various regions of southern Italy colonized by the Greeks, notably Apulia, predominated. This output makes use of many of the same mythological themes as Attic ware, but it also reflects a strong local interest in the theater. After about 300 BCE, figure scenes disappear entirely to make way for the largely plain wares of the Hellenistic period.

BELOW: A rare example of classical Greek wall-painting comes from the "Tomb of the Diver," a young man's grave dating from ca. 480 BCE found at the Greek colony of Poseidonia (Paestum) in southern Italy. The inside of the travertine tomb-chamber is decorated with painted stucco; the four walls depict a symposium scene, a detail of which is shown here, while the ceiling shows a diver plunging into the sea.

GEOMETRIC MOTIFS

The painted decoration on pottery of the protogeometric (1100–900 BCE) and geometric periods (900–700 BCE) at first consisted purely of patterns, from concentric circles to more elaborate motifs, such as the swastika, the maeander ("Greek key pattern"), quatrefoil, cross-hatched triangles, lozenge chains, and parallel zigzag patterns (above). Occasional stylized animal and human figures began to appear ca. 900 BCE, but more complex scenes developed from ca. 770 BCE—ones that represented such popular themes as battles and shipwrecks. The most striking pieces are the enormous kraters and amphoras used as grave markers, which might be as much as 5 feet (1.5 m) high. These are decorated all over with geometric motifs, with a panel or an extended frieze depicting mourners gathered around the body at the laying-out (see opposite) or accompanying the funeral procession. Long after the geometric period, motifs such as the maeander continued to be used for borders on both black- and red-figure painted pottery.

THE WORLD OF THE HELLENES

LEFT: The Mani peninsula in the southern Peloponnese has some of the wildest landscapes in Greece. In antiquity this region was part of Sparta's territory, and Cape Matapan, pictured here, was known as Cape Tainaron.

RIGHT: Coinage appeared in eastern Greece ca. 600 BCE and soon spread across the Greek world. The designs on a coin usually make symbolic reference to the state by which it was issued, as on this Athenian silver tetradrachm of ca. 440 BCE, decorated with the head of the city's patron goddess Athene.

The world of the Greeks extended well beyond modern Greece to include all the Aegean islands and cities around the coast of what is now Turkey, with colonies that stretched from the western Mediterranean to the Black Sea. These widely scattered communities were united by what Herodotus called "Greekness, being of the same blood and language, with shared shrines of the gods and sacrifices, and the same established ways of life." This core of shared religious beliefs and practices can be seen at the Panhellenic sanctuaries, such as Olympia and Delphi, where people from all over the Greek world came to compete in the Games or to consult the oracle. A common language facilitated communication and reinforced many shared cultural values, reflected in a body of Greek literary and artistic traditions.

GREECE AND THE CITY-STATE

Despite the unifying cultural factors, at the political level ancient Greece was fragmented into several hundred autonomous city-states, which were more often at war with one another than united. This division arose at least in part from the landscape: the mainland is riven by high mountain ranges in the Peloponnese and northern Greece, while the population was dispersed over this terrain and the 100-plus inhabited islands. Two main forms of political organization evolved within this fragmented land, the *ethnos* (people) and the *polis* (city-state). An *ethnos* consisted of a population scattered over an extensive territory in villages loosely bound by political affiliations—this tribal kind of organization was common in northern and western Greece (for example, the Thessalians, Epirots, and Aetolians) and in

parts of the Peloponnese (Arcadians, Achaeans). A *polis* was an autonomous political community of people living in a territory that included both a rural area with villages and (usually) a more built-up urban center called an *astu* (town). The conventional translation of *polis* as "city-state" is more abstract than the Greek term, which refers as much to the people as to the place—the Greeks always spoke of "the Corinthians" or "the Thebans," rather than "Corinth" or "Thebes." The majority of *poleis* were quite small, with citizen populations in the hundreds rather than the thousands and territories of less than 40 square miles (100 sq km); the vast territories of Athens (1,000 square miles; 2,600 sq km) and Sparta (more than 2,000 square miles; 5,200 sq km) were exceptional.

LEFT: **Hoplite warfare between Greek states is represented on this early Corinthian jug (*olpe*), known as the "Chigi Vase," which dates from ca. 650 BCE. Use of color and incised detail draw the viewer's attention to the opposing armies' overlapping shields, a key feature of the phalanx formation. The ranks advance in time to the music of the *aulos* (double pipe), played by a young boy.**

The work of Aristotle is an important source of information on the variety of systems by which the *poleis* were governed. In the second half of the fourth century BCE Aristotle's school undertook a huge research project to collect the constitutions (*politeiai*) of 158 Greek states, covering the full range of possible systems: traditional monarchy, tyranny, aristocratic oligarchy, and democracy. On the basis of these case-studies, Aristotle's *Politics* sets out to establish what kind of constitution is best, both in theory and in practice—he is just as critical of the famed democracy of Athens as he is of other systems, and concludes that in fact the best form of government is one made up of a mixture of democratic and oligarchic elements. In addition to the *Politics* itself, we have surviving fragments of the constitutions of more than 80 individual states, and an almost complete account of the *politeia* of the Athenians.

Despite its emblematic status, Athens was not always a democracy. Mythology includes stories about a succession of early kings, ending with Theseus, whom later

ABOVE: **Even today Athens is dominated by its Akropolis, an outcrop of rock that provides a natural defensive position. Here we see the entrance to the Akropolis, marked by the remains of the Periklean Propylaia and temple of Athene Nike (see pages 70–71), viewed from the Areopagos ("Hill of Ares") a little to the northwest.**

BELOW: The Athenians went to great lengths to ensure the impartiality of their democratic institutions—this device is a machine for the random allocation of jurors to the law courts. Tickets inscribed with a citizen's name were slotted into the notches; a random mixture of black and white pebbles was then dropped down a hollow bronze tube to the left. Only jurors whose names appeared on tickets inserted in the rows marked by a white pebble would sit in court that day.

writers credited with the unlikely act of handing over power to "the people." In the seventh century BCE this power was restricted to a number of aristocratic families, from among whom nine magistrates (archons) were chosen each year to preside over community decision-making, in conjunction with the Areopagus council made up of ex-archons. At the beginning of the sixth century BCE the archonship was opened up to a wider social group and a raft of laws was passed, traditionally attributed to Solon, ensuring some basic rights for all citizens. This still oligarchic system was interrupted for much of the second half of the century by the tyranny of Peisistratos and his sons, although they left the archonship intact. More representative government began to emerge with Kleisthenes' reforms in 508–507 BCE, which reorganized the citizen body into ten tribes, each consisting of three *trittyes* ("thirds") and

Spartan soldiers traditionally wore long hair and red cloaks, in the belief that it made them look more terrifying to their opponents in battle. This bronze statuette dating from ca. 500 BCE depicts a Spartan warrior with his hair carefully dressed. His cloak is wrapped tightly around him and he is wearing a Corinthian-type helmet with an unusually angled crest.

made up of a number of *demes* (villages). This broke up the territorial units on which the power of the old aristocratic families had been based, and it provided a new basis for political organization. By the middle of the fifth century BCE all the institutions of democracy proper were in place, crucially the assembly (*ekklesia*) and the council (*boule*). The council comprised 500 members, each of whom held office for one year; 50 members were selected by lot from each tribe. Each tribal group presided in turn for one month of the ten-month civic year. The council prepared measures for discussion and had executive responsibilities, but the ultimate decision-making power lay with the assembly of all citizens (see page 32), *the* characteristic feature of ancient democracy.

After Athens, the state about whose political organization we know most is Sparta—in addition to Aristotle's work, we have a complete *politeia* of the Spartans from the early fourth century BCE, attributed to Xenophon. Unusually, Sparta had a dual kingship, which was hereditary within the Agiad and Eurypontid families, some members of whom exercised a considerable degree of power, especially as military commanders. However, their power was tempered by the authority of the *gerousia*, a council of 28 elders (*gerontes*) whose members had to be aged over 60 but were elected for life. In addition, a board of five magistrates (*ephors*) is supposed to have been instituted at some point in the archaic period with the express purpose of curbing the power of the kings; the ephorate was open to all citizens and elected on an annual basis. Finally, there was an assembly (*apella*) that elected people to the ephorate and *gerousia*, and voted on propositions prepared by these two bodies. This unique combination of dual kingship with oligarchic and democratic elements presided over a Sparta whose military supremacy remained unquestioned until 371 BCE.

THE WINE-DARK SEA

Many of the city-states were divided from one another by the sea, but paradoxi-

cally the sea provided the easiest means of communication and trade—whoever had

control over the sea bolstered their political power. The importance of the sea to

Greek life is reflected in marine motifs, which appear in art of all periods. They

range from shells (left and right), to sea creatures and stylized waves (above), or the

octopus and seaweed on this Minoan pilgrim flask, ca. 1500 BCE, from Crete (oppo-

site). In Homer the sea is often described as "wine-dark," a traditional formula for

the sea at dawn or sunset, or under the storm clouds of a lowering sky.

CITIZENS, WOMEN, AND SLAVES

E ven in the most democratic of Greek states, the rule of "the people" was restricted to male citizens, which meant only a small proportion of the actual population. Criteria for citizenship were strict: at Athens, it was necessary to have a citizen father, and from 451 BCE the mother too had to belong to a citizen family. In a democratic state such as classical Athens the citizen's primary right and responsibility was participation in government (see page 29). Citizens also formed the core of any state's fighting force. At Athens full-time military service was compulsory for *ephebes*, citizen youths aged 18–20, while at Sparta a strict regime of military training began for boys at the age of seven and extended throughout the citizen's life.

A wide range of wealth and social status was possible within the citizen class of Athens, although the only respectable source of income was that derived from land. In his *Oikonomikos* ("Household Management") Xenophon paints the picture of a wealthy landowner living in Athens and riding out of the city each day to supervise his estate. Smaller-scale farmers would have lived and worked on their properties in the Attic countryside; poorer citizens without land could join the navy as oarsmen or practice a craft such as pottery or metalwork. Many commercial activities were in the hands of the metics, free men from other states resident in Athens. Metics were prohibited from owning land and had no political rights, but they were recognized as free men, were protected by the laws, paid taxes, and could be called on to serve in the army.

A number of leisure pursuits were especially associated with the established aristocratic families. Hunting and regular physical exercise were important elements in a wealthy youth's education. Young men exercised naked (*gymnos*) at the gymnasium, which led to its association with homosexual romance—the ideal

relationship for the Athenian aristocrat was one between a man in his twenties and a beautiful teenage boy. Such relationships are discussed in Plato's *Symposium*, our most extensive account of the kind of highly formalized drinking party enjoyed by upper-class men.

The wives and daughters of male citizens were not citizens in their own right, as they had no political role, but they were protected by the laws and had a number of religious privileges. At Athens the generally accepted ideal was for the women of the household to live a sequestered life, only emerging for the occasional religious festival or funeral. However, there is reason to believe that women visited each other in their homes, and women past child-bearing age seem to have had more freedom of movement. Women from poorer families almost certainly had to leave the house to perform daily tasks that in wealthier homes were delegated to slaves, such as fetching water and shopping, and some sold goods in the market. In well-off households a woman's major role would have been in managing the domestic slaves,

LEFT: This Attic *lekythos* uses the white-ground technique, which flourished ca. 470–400 BCE and was used especially to produce objects intended for burial with the dead. It presents the image of the ideal citizen wife: a woman seated in a domestic interior, with a basket of wool at her side. The label to the right of the woman's face reads *kale*, meaning "beautiful."

but women of all economic classes were expected to devote much of their time to childcare, since the bearing of citizen sons was a wife's most important duty.

The life of citizens all over Greece was predicated on the existence of slavery. The Spartans had a large population of helots, or state-owned serfs, who farmed the land; elsewhere, most slaves belonged to individual households. It is estimated that slaves, obtained through war, piracy, or direct trade with slavers among the barbarian peoples, made up 25–30 percent of the population of classical Athens. The daily life of many slaves was probably not very different from that of a poor citizen or metic—slave craftsmen often worked alongside free artisans, while female domestic slaves shared their mistresses' tasks—although much harsher conditions were endured by agricultural slaves and those who worked in the silver mines at Laurion. Not only slave women but young girls and boys were liable to fall victim to sexual exploitation. A slave's well-being was entirely at the owner's discretion, and legally a slave could only bear witness under torture. However, a more humane master might manumit a slave (to metic status) as a reward for good service, and some slaves who worked outside the household, for example as skilled craftsmen, were allowed to keep a proportion of their earnings, with which they might eventually buy their freedom.

BELOW: This 6th-century BCE terracotta model, found at Thebes in Boiotia, depicts four women kneading dough, their work enlivened by the music of an *aulos*-player. They could be the slaves of a wealthy household, or workers in a commercial bakery.

GREEKS AND BARBARIANS

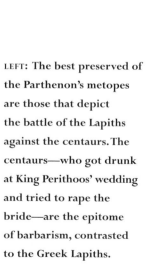

The internal divisions of society provided one set of oppositions by which the Greeks defined themselves (citizen/non-citizen, male/female, slave/free), and affiliation to an *ethnos* or *polis* (Athenian/Corinthian) another. But over and above these there developed an essential distinction between Greeks and non-Greeks. The Greek language was fundamental to the Greeks' self-definition in opposition to the barbarians (*barbaroi*), whose mocked "ba-ba-ba" languages were so incomprehensible. Speaking Greek was a necessary qualification for participation in the Olympic Games and initiation into the Eleusinian Mysteries (see pages 122–3 and 126–7). The idea of a common Greek identity is not very apparent from a study of archaic literature, but increasing numbers of non-Greek slaves in sixth-century BCE Athens contributed to a growing awareness of racial difference. However, the crucial impetus for the "invention of the barbarian" (as it has been called) was provided by the Persian Wars of 490 and 480–479 BCE. In the aftermath of the successful repulsion of the Persians by a coalition of Greek states, Athens formed the Delian League, and justified her leadership of it by emphasizing the need for Greek unity against the common enemy.

LEFT: The best preserved of the Parthenon's metopes are those that depict the battle of the Lapiths against the centaurs. The centaurs—who got drunk at King Perithoos' wedding and tried to rape the bride—are the epitome of barbarism, contrasted to the Greek Lapiths.

The defining feature of the barbarian was said to be a lack of *logos*, not just "speech," but the ability to reason, and with it the ability to have political freedom—Aristotle went so far as to state that barbarians were able to endure despotic rule because they were "naturally more slavish in their disposition than the Greeks." All kinds of negative characteristics were said to be typical of the barbarian: a lack of self-control in regards to food, drink, and sex; a penchant for undiluted wine and emotional music; disregard for the rules of hospitality; cowardliness; and effeminacy of clothing, such as excessive finery and trousers. All of these are referred to in Aeschylus' tragedy the *Persians*, performed in 472 BCE, which began a long tradition of representing the Persians as barbarians *par excellence*. Various mythological characters were also recruited to represent barbarity, and sometimes these were explicitly equated with the Persians. The Trojan prince Paris, for example, appears in Persian costume in a vase-painting from the mid-fifth century BCE, underlining the barbarity of his abduction of Helen from his Spartan host Menelaos, and his use of the coward's weapon, the bow. The ensuing Trojan War was also easy to equate with the Persian Wars, since both conflicts involved the combined effort of Greek states against an eastern threat. The "Greek-versus-barbarian" theme is strongly represented by the metopes in the sculptural program of the Parthenon, which (exceptionally) decorate all four sides of the building. While the gods fighting the giants (east) and the Trojan War (north) illustrate Greek civilization in general pitted against barbarity, the Amazons are overcome by the Athenians in particular, led by their legendary king Theseus (west), who also lends a hand against the centaurs (south).

ABOVE: **This Attic red-figure cup, dated ca. 460 BCE, perfectly displays the contrast between Greek and barbarian: the quintessentially Greek hoplite (right) overcomes a soldier in distinctively Persian dress, including patterned sleeved top and trousers, and the Persian cap.**

THE GREEK DIASPORA

Despite their attitudes toward barbarians, in practice many Greeks found themselves living in close proximity to other cultures due to colonization. The earliest colony to be established was Pithecussae, on Ischia in the Bay of Naples, founded ca. 770 BCE by settlers from the Euboian city of Chalkis. This was soon followed by further foundations at Cumae and Naples itself, and on Sicily, where some colonies even went on to found satellite colonies of their own—in the mid-eighth century BCE Leontini, for example, was founded by Naxos, itself recently founded by Chalkidians. Southern Italy and Sicily continued to be a popular destination for colonists in the seventh and early sixth centuries BCE, to the extent that the Romans later called the region *Magna Graecia* ("Greater Greece"), and Greek dialects may still be heard in some areas to this day. A few colonists ventured even farther west, to Massilia (Marseilles) founded ca. 600 BCE by the people of Phokaia (Asia Minor), who were also responsible for colonies in Italy and Corsica. Others went north, settling in Chalkidiki, along the north coast of the Aegean, all around the Propontis, and the Black Sea. In the southeastern Mediterranean, the foundation of Cyrene is well documented. The settlements at Al Mina in Syria and Naukratis in the Nile Delta did not have the status of independent cities, but were important trading posts (*emporia*) based on ports, where Greeks from various cities had economic and religious rights through the goodwill of existing local powers.

All this dispersion of people had important consequences. The Greeks brought with them a "city way of life," but were in their turn influenced by the indigenous societies. The tensions of the relationship are often revealed by a foundation myth that

LEFT: Sea battles and ship-wrecks are popular themes in late geometric and archaic vase-painting, reflecting the perils encountered by early Greek travelers. Here a merchant-ship (left) is attacked by a battleship full of armed men. The krater, made ca. 650 BCE, was found in Etruria but is signed in Greek by the potter Aristonothos ("best bastard"), who probably worked in one of the Greek colonies in southern Italy or Sicily.

explained how the newcomers came to be there. At Massilia, for instance, a visiting Phokaian is supposed to have been picked out at a banquet by the daughter of a local king to be her husband. Intermarriage between Greeks and locals must in fact have been quite common, since the original colonizing parties do not usually seem to have included women. This localized two-way cultural influence would have had wider consequences, as the colonies opened up new trade routes. The new cities also had a capacity for innovation. At Lokri Epizephyri in southern Italy, Zaleukos is reputed to be the author of the earliest written law code ca. 650 BCE. Megara Hyblaea, on the east coast of Sicily, is one of the earliest examples of Greek town planning, with a regular street grid laid out around an *agora* in the later seventh century. Other Sicilian cities produced famous men of letters, such as the sixth-century BCE lyric poet Stesichoros from Himera, and the sophist Gorgias (ca. 485–380 BCE) from Leontini.

BELOW: The four-horse chariot and warriors here are a detail from the neck of the massive bronze bowl known as the "Vix Krater." It was made ca. 540 BCE at Sparta, but was found in the grave of a Celtic princess in northern Burgundy, at a strategic point on the tin route from Britain to Marseilles. The bowl was probably a gift from Greek traders to the local chieftain.

"FROGS AROUND A POND"

By the fourth century BCE there were so many Greek colonies scattered around the Mediterranean that Plato could describe them as being "like frogs around a pond." The wealth of the early settlements in southern Italy and Sicily can be seen in their monuments, which are some of the most impressive in the Greek world. The first temple of Hera at Poseidonia (Paestum), built ca. 550 BCE, is notable for its size (nine columns by eighteen) and a series of 40 metopes depicting the exploits of Herakles and other heroes. Selinunte (ancient Selinus) in southwestern Sicily boasts no fewer than seven temples, the oldest of which were decorated with striking archaic metopes, now in the museum in Palermo, that feature Europa being transported across the sea by Zeus, Perseus beheading Medusa, and Herakles carrying the Kerkopes.

Also in southern Sicily, Agrigento (ancient Akragas, or Latin Agrigentum) likewise has multiple temples, including the Temple of Concord (right). This was built ca. 430 BCE and owes its remarkable state of preservation to its conversion into a Christian church in the sixth century CE—arches were cut through the inner walls of the temple, but otherwise it was incorporated more or less intact. It is an excellent example of the Doric order, with the canonical six by thirteen columns and architectural refinements, although its pediments and metopes are bare of sculpture. The attribution of the temple to Concord is a modern one based on a Roman inscription found nearby—it is much more likely to have been dedicated to one of the major Olympian gods (see pages 48–79), as are the neighboring temples of Hera and Herakles.

PHILOSOPHERS AND SCIENTISTS

The western colonies were associated with some of Greece's great thinkers—Akragas was birthplace of the philosophers Anaxagoras (ca. 500–428 BCE) and Empedocles (ca. 492–432 BCE). Pythagoras of Samos immigrated to Croton in southern Italy ca. 530 BCE, where he made important discoveries in mathematics, astronomy, and music, and founded the Pythagorean sect, which advocated a belief in the transmigration of souls. Parmenides (ca. 515–450 BCE) founded his philosophical school at Elea, just south of Poseidonia (Paestum), where Zeno (born ca. 490 BCE) wrote his famous paradoxes. The earliest developments in rational thought, however, were in the Ionian cities of Asia Minor, beginning with the philosophers Thales (ca. 640–550 BCE), Anaximander (died ca. 547 BCE), and Anaximenes (fl. 546– 525 BCE) of Miletos, who laid the foundations for Greek geometry, astronomy, and cosmology, and wrote the first prose treaties, "On the Nature of Things," starting a long tradition of Greek natural philosophy. The ideas of the three Milesian philosophers were disseminated to the west via the poetry of Xenophanes of Colophon (ca. 570–475 BCE), and later popularized by the itinerant lecturers known as the Sophists.

These philosophers are referred to today as the "Presocratics," reflecting the importance of Socrates (469–399 BCE) himself. He never wrote down his ideas, but developed them through dialogues with his pupils at Athens, whom he taught to pursue the truth through rational enquiry. Socrates' philosophy is known to us especially through the writings of Plato (ca. 429–347 BCE), who went on to develop his own

LEFT: Portraits of philosophers and other intellectuals were popular in the Hellenistic period, usually combining a degree of individualizing realism with standard features expressive of their role. This portrait of Chrysippos, who was head of the Stoic school of philosophy from 232 until his death in 206 BCE, contrasts the external decay of an aging body with the inner vigor of the mind. This is a Roman-period copy, but the original was probably made in Chrysippos' lifetime.

RIGHT: The octagonal Tower of the Winds, or Horologion ("Clock"), in Athens was designed by Andronikos of Kyrrhos, a Macedonian astronomer, ca. 150–25 BCE. It combined sundials and a weather-vane with a *klepsydra* (water clock), powered by a stream that filled the semicircular reservoir attached to the south face of the tower. Around the top, each face of the tower is decorated with a relief representing one of the eight winds in personified form.

ideas in such influential works as the *Republic*, and founded the Academy, the first of a number of philosophical schools at Athens. Aristotle of Stageira (384–322 BCE) studied there, and later, after several years teaching the future Alexander the Great at the Macedonian court at Pella, established his own school at Athens, the Lyceum. Diogenes of Sinope (ca. 403–324 BCE) came to Athens around 362 BCE, where he practiced a way of life that included the rejection of material possessions and all forms of culture. This extreme behavior earned his followers the nickname Cynics ("dog-like"). Zeno of Citium (335–263 BCE) came to Athens in 313 BCE. He taught in the Agora's Painted Stoa, hence the name Stoic for his school of philosophy. Epicurus of Samos (ca. 341–270 BCE) established a secluded community of pupils at Athens around 306 BCE, which was known as "the Garden."

Many of the philosophers propounded scientific theories, but only limited use was made of practical experimentation. In the field of medicine, the treatises attributed to Hippokrates of Kos (ca. 460–377 BCE) are based on the methodical observation of symptoms, but Herophilos of Chalcedon (ca. 330–260 BCE) and Erasistratos of Kios (ca. 315–240 BCE) were the first known to have dissected human corpses for the study of anatomy. In the field of engineering, eminently practical experiments were carried out by Archimedes (ca. 287–212/211 BCE), whose war machines were used to defend his native Syracuse when it was besieged by the Romans in 213–211 BCE, although the city eventually fell and Archimedes himself died during the siege.

POETS AND ARTISTS

The earliest Greek poetry was oral in form, and was recited or sung directly to an audience, as evoked in Homer's *Odyssey* (ca. 700 BCE), in which the *aoidos* (singer-poet) provides after-dinner entertainment in wealthy households. In Hesiod's epics (also ca. 700 BCE), autobiographical passages show that the *aoidos* might travel great distances in order to perform at public occasions, and that competition between rival poets was expected. During the sixth century BCE it became common for itinerant rhapsodes ("stitchers of song") to compete in the recitation of Homer's poems and other traditional epics at religious festivals all over the Greek world.

Smaller-scale poems collectively known as "lyric" were also popular in the archaic period. These might be performed by the poet himself at a private dinner, to the accompaniment of the lyre, or by a chorus in the more public context of a festival. Much lyric was clearly composed to commission, such as Sappho's wedding songs or Pindar's odes for victorious athletes. Poets of the classical period continued to compete in public, especially in the media of tragedy and comedy, where both solo speech and choral song were in verse. Poets of the Hellenistic period made use of traditional forms, such as that used in Apollonius of Rhodes' epic *Argonautica*, but many were now writing for a public who would read, rather than

LEFT: This "portrait" of Homer was made at least 500 years after the poet's death. It reflects a Hellenistic ideal of what the great man ought to have looked like: aged and blind, with a furrowed brow and altogether otherworldly expression, all redolent of the wisdom, intensity, and inspiration needed to write such great epics as the *Iliad* and *Odyssey*.

listen to, their work (see pages 46–7). This is reflected, for example, in the self-conscious academicism of Callimachus, and the rise to popularity of the short, witty epigram.

Artists dealing with material media were generally not as well respected as the poets. The only artists to be considered worth writing about by ancient authors were sculptors (of free-standing works) and monumental painters—Pliny the Elder devotes a few chapters of his *Natural History* to listing the "masters" and their works, with occasional anecdotes about their lives. A few famous individuals moved in influential circles, such as the sculptor Pheidias, who was rumored to have procured free-born women for Perikles' enjoyment on the Parthenon building site. Alexander the Great is supposed to have handed over his favorite mistress Pankaspe to the painter Apelles, who had fallen in love with her while working on her nude portrait. A few artists were even able to make large fortunes, like the fourth-century BCE painter Zeuxis, who reputedly showed off his wealth by wearing a cloak with his name embroidered in gold thread.

However, even the greatest artists were liable to the prejudice against working with one's hands: "it does not necessarily follow that, if a work is pleasing because of its beauty, the man who made it is worthy of our serious attention" (Plutarch). As for the creators of relief sculpture, and of pottery and its painted decoration, they are scarcely even mentioned in ancient literature, despite the high skill evident in many surviving works. Our evidence for such artists' status is sketchy, but many were or had been slaves, and it would seem that they were regarded in much the same light as cobblers, blacksmiths, and other artisans.

LEFT: This *psykter* (wine-cooler) painted by Smikros ca. 510 BCE depicts a fellow vase-painter labeled "Euphronios" talking to "Leagros," a youth renowned as being the foremost beauty of his day, and courted by the richest men in Athens. Euphronios in turn painted Smikros reclining at a symposium, so the improbable combination may be part of a running joke.

THE ART OF WRITING

reek philosophers, poets, and artists all made use of writing. The art was already known to the Minoans and Mycenaeans, although they seem to have used it primarily for bureacratic rather than literary purposes. The Minoan syllabic script known as Linear A has yet to be decoded, but the Mycenaean Linear B was deciphered in 1952 by Michael Ventris and John Chadwick, who identified it as an early form of Greek. Use of Linear B disappeared with the collapse of the Mycenaean palaces, but the language it recorded continued to be spoken, and writing was re-introduced in the early eighth century BCE using an alphabetic script borrowed from the Phoenicians. At first this script was employed for simple tasks such as marking ownership, but it soon began to be used for recording all kinds of information that had formerly been transmitted orally.

Writing had a profound effect on Greek thought, allowing poetry to be composed and memorized in a completely different way—Homer's epics may have been written down as early as 700 BCE—and facilitating the development of prose, which was to become the primary medium for such "rational" disciplines as philosophy (see pages 42–3) and history.

Writing is widely used on decorated pottery of all types from the seventh century BCE onward, the most common words to be inscribed being the names of mythological characters, although there is no obvious rule governing the inclusion or omission of such labels. In addition to name-labels, two kinds of

RIGHT: This Attic red-figure cup of ca. 490 BCE displays all three of the commonest types of inscription. The mythological characters are named as "Eos" and "Memnon," the winged goddess of Dawn and her son. To the right are the signatures of the potter and the painter: "Kaliades *epoiesen*" ("Kaliades made") and "Douris *egrapsen*" ("Douris painted"). To the left a label declares a youth to be handsome: "Hermogenes kalos."

signature became standard in Attic black- and red-figure pieces: the potter's (*X epoiesen*, or "X made") and the painter's (*X egrapsen*, or "X painted"). Signing one's work is suggestive of some artistic self-awareness, although again the practice is far from universal—many of the finest works remain unsigned. A final type of inscription that is confined to Attic pottery of ca. 550–450 BCE is the "*kalos* name." Labels such as *Leagros kalos*, "Leagros [is] handsome" reflect the upper-class predilection for beautiful youths; several hundred names appear in this way, although some are much more popular than others.

Inscriptions carved in stone have provided scholars with some extremely useful evidence about Greek cultural practices. The bases of statues often bear an inscription naming the figure depicted and the sculptor who made it. The name of the dedicator may also be added in the case of statues or votive reliefs offered to the gods; grave *stelai* usually bear at least the name of the deceased and sometimes a longer epitaph. Other stelai were erected specifically to carry inscriptions recording decisions of the council and assembly, financial accounts and inventories, festival calendars, and religious regulations. This kind of publication, which rendered records both permanent and easily verifiable, was especially typical of democratic states such as Athens, reflecting an ideological concern with accountability.

ABOVE: The "Parian Marble," a stele inscribed on the island of Paros, is a document that has had a major impact on our understanding of Greek chronology. "Starting from Kekrops, the first king of Athens," it lists the dates of a wide selection of political and cultural events down to 264/263 BCE, presumably the date of composition.

THE GODS OF OLYMPOS

The Olympian gods were immortal; each was thought of as coming into existence at a specific point in mythological time, and several have complex birth stories. Much about the gods' characters and lives was established by ca. 700 BCE in the poems of Homer and Hesiod, although more details were elaborated by later writers, sculptors, and painters. Some of the earliest stories portray the Greek deities as surprisingly human—"Homer and Hesiod have attributed all things to the gods which are things of shame and reproach among men … ," complained the sixth-century BCE philosopher Xenophanes. It is one of the central paradoxes of Greek thought that such myths could coexist with daily demonstrations of reverence by ordinary individuals, family groups, and the state, in the form of prayers, sacrifices, and dedications.

LEFT: In art the god Apollo is consistently represented as a beautiful, often naked, youth. The late-Hellenistic bronze statuette from Benevento known as the "Piombino Apollo," the head of which is shown here, imitates the style of an archaic *kouros*, with short but stylized hair and sharply delineated brows; the eyes would have been inlaid.

ABOVE: Hesiod describes Eros, love personified, as one of the primordial elements. Later writers make Eros the son of Aphrodite and Ares, and this Hellenistic terracotta statuette is typical of the ubiquitous image of the slightly mischievous winged boy.

CHILDREN OF CHAOS: TITANS AND OLYMPIANS

Hesiod's epic poem the *Theogony* is a systematic account of the "births of the gods," and of the Greek "Succession Myth," which charts the establishment of the Olympians' rule, and which has close parallels in Hittite and Mesopotamian myth.

In the beginning, according to the *Theogony*, was Chaos, followed by Earth (Ge or Gaia), Eros, and Tartaros, the lowest part of the Underworld. Earth gave birth to Heaven (Ouranos), to whom she then bore the twelve "Titans," as well as Ocean, the one-eyed Cyclopes, and the Hundred-Handed monsters Kottos, Briareos, and Gyges. Heaven hated his children and hid them away until one day Earth made a flint sickle, which the youngest of the Titans, Kronos ("the crooked-planning"), used to castrate his father; from the blood that fell on Earth were born the giants and the Furies, while the genitals produced Aphrodite (see pages 66–7). Kronos then lay with his Titan sister Rheia, who bore him Hestia, Demeter, Hera, Hades, and Poseidon, but, jealous of his position as king of the gods, Kronos swallowed each child as it was born. When a sixth child, Zeus, was due, Rheia sought help from her mother Earth, who hid the baby in a remote cave on the Cretan Mount Dikte and gave Kronos instead a stone wrapped in swaddling clothes. Zeus grew up and came out of hiding to overthrow his father, who was induced to vomit up Zeus' five swallowed siblings.

Kronos' Titan brothers went to war against Zeus and his siblings, whose home was Mount Olympos. After ten years of a war known as the Titanomachy ("battle of the Titans"), the Olympians were victorious, and the Titans were forever imprisoned in Tartaros. Hesiod presents this victory as establishing Zeus' position as king of the gods, although Homer and others refer to a drawing of lots in which Zeus received power over the heavens, Poseidon over the sea, and Hades over the

Underworld. Zeus' authority was later challenged by the monstrous Typhoeus or Typhon, youngest son of Earth; he too was overcome and consigned to Tartaros. The Olympians were eventually able to multiply in peace for a while, before their supremacy was challenged by the giants; according to some, the gods only won the battle with the help of Herakles. The Gigantomachy is not mentioned in epic poetry, but it appears in art from the mid-sixth century BCE onward, and is an especially popular subject for archaic architectural sculpture, where it symbolizes the triumph of Olympian Order over the forces of Chaos.

ABOVE: A detail from the north frieze of the Siphnian Treasury at Delphi, ca. 525 BCE, depicts the Gigantomachy. Here we see Apollo and Artemis pursuing one giant (far right), while a lion, harnessed to pull the chariot of the goddess Themis, attacks another. The giants look like ordinary hoplite soldiers.

OLYMPOS, SEAT OF THE GODS

In poetry the home of the gods is consistently referred to as Olympos, but it is not entirely clear how this place was imagined. According to the *Iliad*, the gods have houses there, built by Hephaistos, where they feast to the music of Apollo's lyre and the singing of the Muses. The site seems to be a mountain, as it has "peaks" and "ridges" and is occasionally even "snowy." On the other hand, the *Odyssey* tells the story of Otos and Ephialtes, giant sons of Poseidon, who threatened to wage war on the gods by piling Mounts Ossa and Pelion on top of Olympos so that they might reach the heavens. This suggests that the gods' abode is somewhere above all these mountains in the sky; when the gods visit the Earth they can be described as coming down either "from Olympos" or "from the Heavens."

We should perhaps not expect consistency in this fantasy world, but when we look at the real Greek landscape it is easy to see how the idea of the gods living on top of an inaccessibly high mountain might have come about. A number of real mountains in Greece are called Olympos, including three in the Peloponnese and one each in Euboia, Cyprus, and Asia Minor. However, the best candidate for identification as the home of the gods is the Mount Olympos (seen here) on the border between Thessaly and Macedonia, which soars to a mighty 9,570 feet (2,917 m). Its two highest peaks, Mytikas ("the Needle") and Stafani (or "the Throne of Zeus"), were not conquered by modern climbers until 1912.

LOUD–THUNDERING ZEUS

A number of standard epithets exist in epic poetry for Zeus (Roman Jupiter), such as "the far-seeing Olympian"; others reflect his position of power ("lord," "king"), or his origins as a weather god ("loud-thundering," "rainy"). However, Zeus is most frequently seen in roles reflecting his concern for human justice, hospitality, and fair treatment for the vulnerable. He was widely worshiped as Zeus Xenios, "of strangers," and Hikesios, "of suppliants"; as Agoraios ("of the market-place") he oversaw public gatherings and fair commerce, and as Herkeios ("of enclo-sures") and Ktesios ("of property") he protected individual households. Although he had no major city-center temples, great importance was attached to his main interstate sanctuaries: in the Peloponnese, where the Panhellenic Games were celebrated in his honor at Olympia and Nemea; and the oracular shrine at Dodona in northwestern Greece.

Zeus' position as strongest of the gods was reflected in his sexual potency, a prolific begetting of offspring earning him the title "father of gods and men." After establishing his rule on Olympos, he took a whole succession of goddesses as his wife: Metis ("Mind"; see page 68); Themis ("Order"), mother of the Seasons and the Fates; the sea-nymph Eurynome, mother of the Graces; his sister Demeter; Mnemosyne ("Memory"), mother of the Muses; and Leto. His sister Hera eventually became his official consort, by whom he had Ares (god of war), Eileithyia (goddess of childbirth), and Hebe ("Youth"). Zeus was often portrayed as rather hen-pecked, but he continued to arouse his wife's fury by his philandering with other goddesses and mortal women, on whom he fathered yet more divine children. Hera was equally incensed by Zeus' one homosexual love interest, the beautiful young Trojan prince Ganymede whom Zeus abducted to Olympos.

RIGHT: **All over the Greek world Zeus is portrayed as a mature, bearded man, often enthroned, as depicted on this Laconian cup by the Naukratis Painter ca. 560 BCE. Zeus is accompanied by his regular animal associate, the eagle. Zeus even assumed the form of an eagle, according to some, when he went in pursuit of Ganymede.**

RIGHT: Zeus is easily recognized in this bronze statuette because he is holding a thunderbolt, his most frequent attribute in art. This piece dates from ca. 470 BCE and comes from Zeus' oldest sanctuary, which Homer refers to as "wintry" Dodona.

THE VENGEFUL QUEEN OF HEAVEN

Hera (the Roman Juno) was portrayed from the *Iliad* onward as constantly ready to cause trouble for her husband's lovers and their offspring. Notably, she prompted Semele to request that Zeus appear to her in all his divine glory, as a consequence of which Semele was burned to death. Hera also persecuted Alkmene's son Herakles throughout his mortal life. Another mortal who suffered Hera's anger was Teiresias, who took Zeus' side in an argument by alleging that women gain nine times more pleasure out of lovemaking than men; for this Hera struck him blind, although Zeus granted him the gift of prophecy as compensation. Although Hera did not herself have any extra-marital affairs, according to Hesiod she conceived Hephaistos without Zeus' assistance. There are also stories of attempted rapes of Hera by the giant Porphyrion and the mortals Endymion and Ixion (see page 110), all thwarted by Zeus.

During the Trojan War Hera and Athene sided with the Greeks in revenge against the Trojan prince Paris, who had chosen Aphrodite as the fairest of the goddesses. At one point in the *Iliad* Hera enlists the help of Aphrodite and the god Sleep in an elaborate seduction scheme to distract Zeus' attention from the battlefield while the Greeks gain the upper hand. This anti-Trojan bias continued in Hera's persecution of Aeneas during his long voyage to Italy, as related in Virgil's *Aeneid*.

Despite her rather negative portrayal in myth, Hera was widely worshiped alongside Zeus as a patron of marriage, and in her own right she was the dedicant of

LEFT: At Athens and elsewhere there was a special "wedding month" (Gamelion), when human marriages were celebrated alongside the "holy wedding" (*hieros gamos*) of Zeus and Hera. On the east frieze of the Parthenon (447–438 BCE), Hera and Zeus are enthroned, facing one another, and Hera holds back her veil in a gesture symbolic of her status as his wife. The young female figure beside Hera may be Iris.

some of the oldest and most important temples in Greece. The first of several temples at Hera's sanctuary on Samos may have been built as early as ca. 800 BCE, while the mid-sixth-century one was reputedly the largest of its day. At Perachora (on the gulf of Corinth) Hera was worshiped from the eighth century onward in two separate temples, as Akraia ("of the headland") and Limenia ("of the harbor"). At Olympia, Hera's late seventh-century temple is considerably older than that of Zeus, and a quadrennial festival was held in her honor, organized by women and with races for girls. The "Argive Heraion," between Argos and Mycenae, was established in the eighth century, but ca. 420–410 BCE it was equipped with a new temple that housed a magnificent gold-and-ivory cult statue by the famous Argive sculptor Polykleitos.

RIGHT: The second temple of Hera at Poseidonia (Paestum), a Greek colony in southern Italy, was built ca. 470–460 BCE. The interior columns of the inner chamber can be clearly seen here, along with an unusually well preserved upper colonnade.

POSEIDON, LORD OF THE SEAS

Repeated mention of Poseidon in the Linear B tablets suggests that he was already important in Mycenaean times, and his association with the sea gave him a special significance for the sea-faring Greeks; the Romans identified him with Neptunus, the Italic god of water. Poseidon's official consort was the sea-nymph Amphitrite, by whom he had the merman Triton and other watery offspring, but, like Zeus, Poseidon had many children as a result of amorous affairs. A strikingly high proportion of these are "baddies," such as the brigands Skiron, Sinis, and Kerkyon who haunted the Saronic Gulf. Odysseus' blinding of his son Polyphemos was punished by years of storm-tossed wanderings at sea, a story that demonstrates Poseidon's dangerous powers. Control over the terrors of the deep is also apparent in the myths of Hesione and Andromeda, both rescued only at the last minute from Poseidon's sea-monsters. Poseidon's power over the sea was matched by an equally terrifying power as god of earthquakes, reflected in his epic epithet Ennosigaios ("Earth-shaker"), and an association with strong land animals. He was sometimes worshiped as Hippios ("of horses"); it was in the form of a horse that he mated with his sister Demeter, begetting the divine horse Areion; he also gave divinely swift horses to his lover Pelops. Poseidon sent a magnificent white bull from the sea as a gift to King Minos, but when Minos failed to

LEFT: This well-known bronze statue, ca. 460–450 BCE, was found on the seabed off Cape Artemision at the northern tip of the Ionic island of Euboia. Although thought by some to represent Zeus, it is just as likely to be his brother Poseidon.

sacrifice it, the god drove Minos' queen Pasiphae mad with desire for the animal, as a result of which the Minotaur was born (later slain by Theseus).

In Homer the Greeks sacrificed to Poseidon on the seashore, and the god's sanctuaries were often within sight of the sea. The Spartans had a sanctuary of Poseidon at Tainaron (modern Cape Matapan) on the southernmost tip of the Peloponnese, while the Athenians had a sanctuary at Cape Sounion (see illustration, below). Poseidon was also worshiped in Athens, despite having lost the competition for the city's patronage (see pages 68–9); on the Akropolis part of the Erechtheion was sacred to him, and the name of the month Posidea implies the existence of an ancient festival in his honor. In a contest for the patronage of Corinth he was more successful: under the Hundred-Handed Briareos' arbitration, the sun-god Helios was awarded the citadel of Upper Corinth and Poseidon took possession of the Isthmos. The sanctuary at the Isthmos hosted local worship from an early date, but in ca. 582 BCE the Corinthians founded the biennial Panhellenic festival, which included the Isthmian Games (see pages 122–3).

BELOW: The temple of Poseidon at Sounion is spectacularly sited on Attica's most southerly headland, where it can be seen by ships far out to sea. It was built ca. 444 BCE to replace an earlier temple that had been destroyed by the Persians in 480. Although only fragments of the new building's frieze survive, it seems to have depicted myths including the exploits of Poseidon's son Theseus (see pages 96–7).

POWERS OF EARTH AND UNDERWORLD

BELOW: The dead were often buried with a coin in their mouth to pay Charon the ferryman's fare to cross the river Styx. On this Attic white-ground *lekythos*, ca. 475–450 BCE, Charon is shown holding a tiny winged soul in his hand.

Zeus' brother Hades ruled over the Underworld (also known as Hades) with his consort Persephone (Roman Proserpina). Both Greeks and Romans called him Pluto, "the Wealthy," in reference to the riches within the earth, and this connection is articulated in his major myth. After Hades abducted Persephone to his home, her mother Demeter (Roman Ceres), goddess of corn, wandered the world searching for her, and while she grieved the earth was barren (see pages 126–7). Eventually Zeus ordered Hades to give Persephone back, but Hades managed to achieve a settlement by which she should spend part of the year with him and part with her mother, her time in the Underworld coinciding with the winter months.

The geography of the Underworld was not precisely worked out by ancient writers, but it was always described as a cold and sunless place, with five rivers: the Styx (the Hateful); the Acheron (River of Woe); the Kokytos (River of Wailing); Phlegethon (River of Flame); and Lethe (River of Forgetfulness). The entrance to Hades was guarded by the monstrous hound Kerberos, variously envisaged as having two, three, or as many as fifty heads. Within the Underworld, the Elysian Fields offered a few blessed mortals an afterlife of ease, while a number of famous wrongdoers suffered eternal punishments in the depths of Tartaros, but the majority of the dead led an insubstantial existence in-between.

Three judges of the dead are sometimes mentioned, Aiakos and the brothers Rhadamanthys and Minos, all of whom had had a reputation for justice during their lives. Harsh punishments were meted out by the Furies (Erinyes), offspring of Heaven's castration (see page 50) and best known for their pursuit of Orestes. They are often represented carrying torches, as is Persephone herself.

RIGHT: Images of the Underworld are especially popular on South Italian vases, such as this monumental krater of ca. 330 BCE, which gives the Underworld Painter his name. Various famous inhabitants of Hades' realm are represented, but at the center (illustrated in this detail) Hades himself is enthroned in his palace with Persephone, who is shown crowned as his queen and holding her trademark torch.

PLANT MOTIFS

Agricultural fertility was so important to the ancient Greeks that it is not surprising plant motifs are ubiquitous in Greek art. The poppy was popular (above, center), as was the wheatsheaf (above, left and right), which recalls the centrality of corn as a symbol in the worship of Demeter at Eleusis. In black- and red-figure vase-painting complex palmette (left and right) and acanthus motifs were developed to provide borders for the main image and to decorate subsidiary zones, such as the neck of an amphora or the space beneath the handles of a krater. Plant motifs are found in architectural sculpture as early as ca. 600 BCE, but became standard with the invention ca. 400 BCE of the Corinthian column capital, made up of acanthus leaves, spirals, and palmettes, a Hellenistic variant of which is shown here (opposite).

EXPLORING THE LIFE, MYTH, AND ART OF ANCIENT GREECE

GUARDIANS OF THE FLAMES

Zeus' eldest sister Hestia plays very little role in myth and is only rarely depicted in art, due to her very close association with the immovable "hearth" (*hestia*)—no other major deity has such a closely defined sphere of influence. Poseidon and Apollo once competed for Hestia's love, but she " ... swore a great oath, which has indeed been fulfilled, touching the head of aegis-bearing Zeus, that she would remain a maiden all her days, noblest of goddesses. So father Zeus gave to her a fine honor instead of marriage, and she has her seat in the middle of the house, taking the best portion" (*Homeric Hymn to Aphrodite*). Hestia was indeed worshiped in every private household, where small offerings of food and drink would be made to her on a daily basis. New members of the family were welcomed with rituals such as the *amphidromia*, in which a five-day-old baby would be "run around" the hearth to signify his or her acceptance into the family. Although she never attained the prominence outside the home of her Roman equivalent Vesta, Hestia was honored at the public hearth that each city maintained in a central temple or civic building, such as the Prytaneion in the Athenian Agora.

Also closely associated with fire is Hera's son Hephaistos (the Roman Vulcan). On his birth Hera, disgusted by his deformed foot, threw him out of Olympos. He was rescued by the sea-nymph Thetis, and later took revenge on his mother by

LEFT: The interior of this Attic red-figure cup by the Antiphon Painter, ca. 480 BCE, depicts a young metalworker making a helmet. In front of him is an anvil, and on the wall behind him hang a range of files and engraving tools.

making her a golden throne with invisible chains. He refused to come and release her from these fetters until Dionysos made him drunk and brought him up to Olympos on a mule, a scene often depicted in Attic vase-painting. Hephaistos was flung from the heavens a second time by Zeus, for taking Hera's side against him, but rescued by the people of Lemnos; in classical times the island's principal town was called Hephaistia and an ancient fire festival was held there. In the *Iliad* and Hesiod Hephaistos is married to one of the Graces, but in the *Odyssey* he is the unlikely husband of Aphrodite herself (see pages 66–7). As the archetypal master-craftsman he supplied all the gods' practical needs, and he is present in any story involving craftsmanship: he fashioned the first woman Pandora; assisted at Athene's birth (see illustration, page 69); cast magnificent new armor for Achilles at Thetis' request; and directed the Cyclopes in his forge beneath Mount Etna in Sicily.

Apart from Lemnos, Hephaistos' only major place of worship was Athens, due to the curious myth in which he tried to rape Athene (see pages 68–9). Both deities were worshiped at Hephaistos' temple in the Agora (see illustration, above), and the Chalkeia ("copper festival") was celebrated in honor of them both. Hephaistos also had a festival of his own, the Hephaisteia, which included a torch race.

ABOVE: **Mainland Greece's best-preserved Doric temple is that of Hephaistos in Athens, situated in the metalworkers' quarter toward the southwest corner of the Agora. Built between ca. 450 and 415 BCE, it housed bronze statues of Hephaistos and Athene by Alkamenes, a pupil of Pheidias. The metopes at the east end depicting the labors of Herakles and Theseus are badly worn, but the mythological battles carved inside both porches can still be seen clearly.**

THE SEA-BORN GODDESS OF LOVE

Aphrodite (Roman Venus) was the goddess of love and fertility, who wielded irresistible power over all living creatures and even the gods. According to Homer, the goddess was the daughter of Zeus and Dione, who was either a Titan or a sea-nymph and was worshiped alongside Zeus as Dodona. In Hesiod's *Theogony*, however, he tells the bizarre story of Aphrodite's birth from Heaven's severed genitals: "Kronos cast these from the land into the surging sea, and so they were borne over the main for a long time, and around them arose a white foam from the immortal flesh, and in it grew a maiden." The waves carried Aphrodite to the island of Kythereia and then to Cyprus, where she was greeted by Eros (Love) and Himeros (Desire) and escorted to the assembly of the gods. Aphrodite's name was thought to derive from the foam (*aphros*) in this story—she was also often referred to as Kythereia, Kypris, or Paphia, and her most ancient sanctuaries were on Cyprus.

In the *Odyssey*, Aphrodite is officially married to Hephaistos, but her regular lover is the war god Ares. Hephaistos gained revenge by catching the pair *in flagrante* by means of a magical invisible net, then calling in the rest of the gods to laugh at their humiliation. Aphrodite nonetheless had several children by Ares, including Eros and Harmonia, who became Kadmos' queen at Thebes. By either Poseidon or the Argonaut Boutes, Aphrodite also gave birth to Eryx, who founded her sanctuary in his eponymous city (modern Erice) in western Sicily. The goddess had another affair with the mortal Anchises, whom she seduced when he was out tending his flocks on Mount Ida outside Troy, and she bore him Aeneas. Throughout the Trojan War she supported the Trojan side, for Aeneas' sake and because of Paris' judgment in her favor. Aphrodite's other great passion was for

LEFT: **Praxiteles' Aphrodite was made for the goddess' sanctuary at Knidos ca. 350 BCE, and was the first full-scale female nude in Greek sculpture. We only have Roman copies to judge it by, often incomplete like this one in the Louvre, but the original prompted ancient writers to lavish praise because of its beauty.**

LEFT: This bronze head of Aphrodite was found at Sattala (modern Sadagh) in eastern Turkey. It dates to the 2nd or 1st century BCE, although it reflects the idealized beauty of the classical and earlier Hellenistic periods.

BELOW: On this gold ring, ca. 350 BCE, Aphrodite is depicted weighing two little Eros figures. The scene, symbolizing some kind of decision in the realm of love, is a light-hearted rework of the scene in the *Iliad* in which Zeus weighs the souls of Achilles and Hektor to decide which of them should die that day.

Adonis, the beautiful youth she shared with Persephone until he was gored to death by a boar; later writers make her the mother of the fertility god Priapos by Dionysos, and of the original hermaphrodite (Hermaphroditos) by Hermes.

The public worship of Aphrodite was sometimes connected with city affairs, as at Athens, where she had the cult title Pandemos ("of all the people"). She was often associated with prostitutes, as at Corinth, where her sanctuary was renowned for its "hospitable young ladies, servants of Persuasion" (Pindar), as many as a thousand of whom were dedicated to Aphrodite's work. She was also worshiped throughout the Greek world in connection with marriage, and at an even more private level by individuals, as beautifully evoked in Sappho's *Hymn to Aphrodite*.

ATHENE THE WISE

Like the virgin goddesses Hestia and Artemis, Athene (Roman Minerva) was immune to Aphrodite's power. Athene's wisdom is explained by her birth story: Zeus married Metis ("Mind") and she duly became pregnant but, on discovering that his wife was destined one day to bear a son greater than his father, Zeus swallowed her. When the child came to term, Hephaistos split open Zeus' head and Athene emerged: "Awe seized all the immortals as they watched; but she sprang from the immortal head and stood before aegis-bearing Zeus, shaking a sharp spear; and great Olympos reeled terribly at the strength of the gray-eyed one; the earth around groaned fearfully; and the sea was moved, stirred up with dark waves … ." (*Homeric Hymn to Athene*).

This image reflects the Athene of Greek art, the war-goddess recognizable by her helmet, spear, and snake-fringed aegis. In addition to her warrior function, however, Athene presided over civilized crafts, especially women's wool-working, but also metalwork and carpentry; she invented the chariot and the horse's bridle, and helped in the building of the first ship and the Trojan Horse. She was patron of various heroes, especially Odysseus "of many wiles," Herakles, and Theseus, and she was a strong supporter of the Greeks in the Trojan War. Her most common epithets were *glaukopis*, "gray-" or "flashing-eyed," and Pallas, perhaps referring to her slaying of the giant Pallas during the Gigantomachy. The "little Pallas" (Palladion) was the name of Athene's statue that guaranteed Troy's safety until it was stolen by the Greeks.

Athene was widely worshiped as Polias or Poliouchos ("of the city" or "city-holding"), and the fortified centers of many cities housed a temple to her. On the Spartan akropolis she was Chalkioikos ("of the bronze

LEFT: **Pheidias' statue of Athene Parthenos stood around 40 feet (12 m) high, and was made of ivory and gold. It portrayed Athene wearing an elaborate helmet and snake-covered aegis, and holding the winged figure of Victory in her hand; her shield, decorated with scenes from battles against Giants and Amazons, rested beside a huge snake that may have represented Erechtheus. Sadly, this magnificent creation is only known to us today through written descriptions and reduced-scale marble copies such as this one, known as the "Minerva with collar," in the Louvre.**

house"), because her temple was decorated with bronze reliefs, while at Argos she was Oxyderkes ("far-seeing"). But she is especially associated with Athens, the city whose name she shares, and their close relationship is elaborated in two major local myths. In the reign of Athens' first king Kekrops, Athene competed with Poseidon for patronage of the city: he offered salt water, but her gift of the olive was preferred. Ever afterward a "sea" and a sacred olive tree were maintained in the Erechtheion (see illustration, page 119), which also housed the ancient wooden statue of Athene Polias, recipient of the robe (*peplos*) presented at the annual Panathenaia festival.

Hephaistos' attempted rape of Athene also occurred in Kekrops' reign: as Athene fled his embraces, Hephaistos' sperm fell on her thigh, which she wiped off in disgust so that it fell to Earth. In due course Earth produced the baby Erichthonios (sometimes called by the name of his grandson Erechtheus), whom Athene took to raise, and he too later became king of Athens. Thus the myth makes it possible for Athene to be the mother of the Athenian people while retaining her prized virginity.

RIGHT: **On this Attic black-figure cup, decorated ca. 560 BCE by Phrynos, the birth of Athene is reduced to its bare essentials: the tiny, but fully armed, figure of Athene emerges from the head of Zeus, who is enthroned and wielding a thunderbolt. His work done, Hephaistos steps away with his axe.**

THE PARTHENON

Athene's most famous temple—seen dominating the Athenian Akropolis in the center of this image—celebrated her status as a virgin (*parthenos*) in its very name, the Parthenon. After the Persian sack of 480 BCE the Akropolis had been left in ruins, but in the early 440s Perikles, the city's foremost general and political leader, instigated a grand program of rebuilding on the Akropolis. The Parthenon, which was constructed between 447 and 438, was the first project to be completed at the site.

With an area of around 100 feet (30 m) by 230 feet (70 m) the Parthenon was the biggest temple on the Greek mainland, and its purpose was to provide a suitably grand home for Pheidias' new statue of Athene Parthenos. An exceptional quantity of architectural sculpture adorned the building's exterior, all of which celebrated the goddess in some way. The pediment at the east end, over the entrance, depicted Athene's birth. The west pediment, of which only fragments survive, portrayed her competition with Poseidon.

The frieze that ran around the inside of the colonnade represents a cavalcade of youths on horseback. The riders are accompanying a procession of people on foot, each of whom is shown leading sacrificial animals (see illustration, page 121), carrying water, or playing musical instruments. At the east end of the temple the procession meets a gathering of seated gods, in the midst of whom a group of mortals handle a folded cloth. There has been a great deal of recent debate about the subject of the frieze, but there is still much to be said for its traditional identification with the Panathenaic procession, culminating with the presentation of the new robe to Athene.

The goddess' civilizing influence can even be seen in the "Greek-versus-barbarian" theme of the metopes (see pages 36–7); the Gigantomachy scenes at the east end echo the scenes that were said to be woven into Athene's robe, depicting "her exploits with Zeus against the giants

APOLLO, LORD OF LIGHT

BELOW: This Attic white-ground *lekythos*, ca. 490 BCE, depicts Muses dancing with castanets while Apollo plays the kithara, a more complex version of the lyre.

Like Athene, Apollo was seen as a civilizing power, the god of prophecy and purification, patron of music, and guardian of flocks. As patron of music he was sometimes called "leader of the Muses," and he often appears in these goddesses' company. His most common epithet was Phoibos ("bright, radiant") and from the fifth century BCE he was identified with the sun god Helios. Apollo was also sometimes identified with Paian, god of healing, but in the *Iliad* he is primarily "the far-shooter" and "lord of the silver bow," whose arrows bring plague on the Greeks for dishonoring his priest: "Phoibos Apollo came down along the peaks of Olympos, angered in his heart, carrying the bow and close-covered quiver on his shoulders; the arrows clanged against the shoulders of the angry god as he moved; and he came down like the night."

Apollo's major sanctuary at Delos, at the center of the Cyclades, was closely linked to the story of his birth, as recounted in the *Homeric Hymn to Apollo*. When Leto was pregnant with Apollo and Artemis by Zeus, fear of Hera's wrath meant that no land would give her shelter, until she reached the tiny island of Delos, which was influenced by the offer of the riches that Apollo's sanctuary would bring. Jealous, as ever, of her husband's infidelity, Hera kept the birth-goddess Eileithyia away for nine days, but on the tenth Leto cast her arms around a palm tree and gave birth to Apollo, who was fed on nectar and ambrosia by Themis. As soon as he tasted the divine food, he precociously announced his future roles: "The kithara will be dear to me, and the curved bow, and I shall proclaim to men the unfailing will of Zeus." The second half of the *Hymn* tells the story of the foundation of Apollo's great oracular sanctuary at Delphi (see pages 130–31). Apollo had no regular consort, but he seduced a number of mortal women, often passing on his skills to their children: Koronis bore him the healing-god Asklepios; Evadne the seer Iamos; and Cyrene a son Aristaios, skilled in healing and prophecy. With other lovers Apollo was less lucky: Daphne turned into a laurel tree to escape him; the Trojan princess Kassandra accepted his gift of prophecy but then rejected his advances, and so was doomed never to be believed; the youth Hyakinthos was tragically killed by Apollo's own discus.

Worship of Apollo was widespread throughout the Greek world. He had a series of oracles along the coast of Asia Minor, notably at Klaros and at Didyma; the latter was housed in a small shrine enclosed within a spectacularly large-scale temple. In the Peloponnese, Apollo was particularly important to the Spartans, who had a very ancient Apollo sanctuary at Amyklai and celebrated two major festivals in his honor, the Karneia and the Hyakinthia. In neighboring Arkadia, Apollo was fêted as Epik-ourios ("protector") in his temple located in the mountains at Bassae. At Athens he was wor-shiped especially as Patroos ("ancestral") Apollo, and at two important festivals: the Apatouria, during which young men were formally admit-ted to the citizen body after cutting their hair for Apollo, and the Thargelia, when "scapegoats" were expelled to purify the city and musical competi-tions were held.

LEFT: The Vatican's "Apollo Belvedere" is a Roman copy of what must have been an important original of ca. 300 BCE, which is sometimes attributed to Leochares of Athens. Like most representations of Apollo, the statue depicts him as a beautiful, naked youth.

ARTEMIS THE HUNTRESS

Artemis (Roman Diana), the virgin goddess of hunting, was Apollo's twin sister who shared his ability with the bow. Sometimes the two acted in concert, especially in defense of their mother Leto's honor: they shot dead the giant Tityos when he tried to rape her, and when Niobe boasted that she was a more prolific mother, the twins promptly killed all of her twelve (or more) children. This close family connection was mirrored in cult—Artemis and Leto were often worshiped within Apollo's sanctuaries. Apollo's identification with the sun was mirrored by Artemis' association with the moon (personified as the goddess Selene).

Homer's *Odyssey* provides the definitive portrait of "arrow-pouring Artemis," who "goes across the mountains, over high Taygetos or Erymanthos, delighting in boars and swift-running deer, and with her play the country-haunting nymphs, daughters of aegis-bearing Zeus." Later writers easily identified Artemis with the Near Eastern mother-goddess Kybele, as well as the huntress-goddesses Britomartis of Crete and Aphaia of Aigina. The huntress is also protector of wild

BELOW: Each plaque of this gold necklace, made in Rhodes ca. 630–620 BCE, depicts Artemis in her typical early archaic form as "Mistress of Animals" (as Homer calls her), with wings and flanked by lions.

RIGHT: This statue of Artemis, which dates from ca. 340–330 BCE, is one of only a few surviving original Greek bronze sculptures. It was found at Piraieus in 1959, as part of a cache of statues—possibly a consignment ready for export that was never shipped because it was overtaken by the Roman sack of the town in 86 BCE.

things; association with the wild was marked at Patrai in the Peloponnese, where the annual festival of Artemis Laphria included an exceptional sacrifice of wild animals and birds, which were driven onto a massive altar and burned alive.

Young humans as well as animals came under Artemis' protection, and she was connected with rites of passage for both girls and boys. At Sparta she was identified with a local goddess Orthia, from whose altar a group of boys would snatch cheeses while others tried to prevent them by wielding whips; it was said that the ancient cult statue enjoyed watching the blood thus spilled, and that the ritual was a "civilized" alternative to human sacrifice. At Artemis' sanctuary at Brauron, in rural Attica, young girls from select Athenian families "played the bear for Artemis," in a ritual that involved dancing and running races. Within the sanctuary there was also a shrine of the heroine Iphigeneia, where the clothes of women who had died in childbirth were dedicated. Artemis' strong connection with childbirth (she was sometimes even identified with Eileith Yia) may in fact be a vestige of her older character as a mother-goddess, but it was explained in antiquity as being due to her anger at loss of virginity. All over Greece girls made placatory sacrifices to Artemis when they were about to leave her sphere for Aphrodite's realm of marriage, and further prayers and offerings were made to dissuade the goddess from inflicting labor pains or even graver dangers during childbirth.

ARTEMIS IN THE EAST

Artemis was commonly worshiped in the Greek cities along the Asia Minor coast, but also by their non-Greek neighbors in Lydia and Lykia. The Lydian capital Sardis lay in the Hermos valley (in what is now western Turkey), near the junction of routes from the coastal cities of Smyrna and Ephesos to inland Anatolia. This strategic position led to the later adoption of Sardis as one of the principal cities of the Seleucid dynasty (see page 15). Under Seleucid rule, Sardis became fully Hellenized, and in the early third century BCE the temple of Artemis (pictured here) was built. At eight columns wide and twenty long, the construction was on a grand scale. The colossal columns were as much as 6 feet, 6 inches (2 m) in diameter and nearly 59 feet (18 m) high, and were topped with particularly ornate Ionic capitals.

The Sardis temple was also known as the temple of Kybele, the Asiatic mother-goddess with whom Artemis seems to have been identified at Ephesos, where her cult statue was covered in what have been variously interpreted as breasts, eggs, or even bull's testicles—all denoting fertility. The temple at Sardis may well have been designed in emulation of Artemis' temple at Ephesos, which had been rebuilt by a team that included the eminent sculptor Skopas after the original burned down in 356 BCE. The original, erected ca. 560–550 BCE, had already been one of the seven wonders of the ancient world, partly financed by the famously rich Lydian king Croesus. The fourth-century BCE replacement was on an even larger scale, around 230 feet (70 m) wide by 440 feet (135 m) long and surrounded by more than 100 columns.

LORDS OF TRANSITION

Two gods who have much in common are Hermes (Roman Mercury) and Dionysos (also known as Bacchus). Both were sons of Zeus, both were concerned with the crossing of boundaries, and both underwent a transformation in their visual image, from the archaic figures of mature, bearded men to a classical and later embodiment as beautiful youths.

ABOVE: Hermes, depicted inside this Attic red-figure cup of ca. 470 BCE, is easily recognized in art by his distinctive attributes. He wears a traveler's sun hat, a cloak, and winged boots, and carries the messenger's staff.

Hermes' mother Maia bore him in a cave in Arkadia, and from earliest infancy the god displayed mischievous cunning. He made the first lyre from a tortoise shell, stole Apollo's cattle, and eventually gave Apollo the lyre in return for becoming divine keeper of herds. This early craftiness was adduced in explanation of Hermes' role as patron of traders and thieves. Hermes' most conspicuous function, however, was as the messenger god, who alone of the Olympians could easily pass between worlds. As guardian of thresholds Hermes was to be found at crossroads and at the entrance to sanctuaries and private houses, especially in the form of the "herm," a square pillar with the god's head and a set of genitals (see illustration, page 116).

When Dionysos' mother Semele was burned to death (see pages 56–7), the child was snatched from her womb and sewn into Zeus' thigh. In due course Dionysos was born, and Hermes delivered the baby to be brought up by the nymphs of Mount Nysa in Asia Minor. Dionysos eventually returned to found his cult in Greece and spread knowledge of the vine, beginning with his mother's native Thebes. The story of the Theban king Pentheus' fatal resistance to Dionysos is the subject of Euripides' *Bacchae*, named after the chorus of the god's female followers, who ripped Pentheus limb from limb in the frenzy of their worship.

RIGHT: The interior of this wine cup, painted by Exekias ca. 540 BCE, is one of the masterpieces of Attic black-figure decoration. When some Tyrrhenian pirates tried to kidnap Dionysos, their ship was flooded with wine, vines and ivy sprouted about the mast, and the god turned into a lion—all of which terrified the crew into jumping overboard. Exekias has depicted the aftermath: Dionysos reclines with a drinking-horn while the former pirates, transformed into dolphins, gambol in the waves.

PRIDE, FATE, AND GLORY

In addition to the many Olympian gods and goddesses, the Greeks revered a host of heroes, most of whom were believed to have lived in the distant past. Many were worshiped with regular rituals at the supposed site of their tomb and known only locally. Some heroes were regarded as founders of their community, a role that was particularly important in the "new" cities established by colonization, while others were considered to have special oracular powers or the ability to heal the sick. Those best known to us are the heroes whose warrior prowess and strange adventures were recounted in epic poetry from Homer and Hesiod onward, while some gained further renown from their representation on the tragic stage of fifth-century BCE Athens.

BELOW: This 4th-century BCE bronze helmet from southern Italy has hinged cheek-pieces, ornamental wings, and a griffin's head, and is embossed to imitate the wearer's eyebrows and a diadem set over his hair.

LEFT: This detail of a Corinthian vase, ca. 600 BCE, depicts a scene that could have come straight from the *Iliad*: a warrior defends his fallen comrade—who lies on the ground, his wound bleeding profusely—against two enemy soldiers.

CHILDREN OF GAIA

In the "Races of Man" myth from Hesiod's poem the *Works and Days*, an age of heroes is fitted into an account of humankind's creation and subsequent decline. The tale recounts that in the beginning the gods created humans as a golden race, the members of which lived an idyllic life with all their needs supplied by a fruitful land. After this came a silver race, who were foolish and neglected to worship the gods, so Zeus replaced them with a third race of bronze, who were so strong and warlike that they destroyed themselves. The only race not characterized by a metal is the fourth, "a more righteous and noble one, the godlike race of hero-men who are called demigods, our predecessors on the boundless Earth." This is the race to which all the great heroes of myth belong, some of whom simply died in battle, although others were granted a life after death. After the heroes came the current race of iron, which "never rests from labor and sorrow by day, nor from perishing by night," and for which Hesiod predicts worse suffering and degeneration in the future.

In a separate story, also told in the *Theogony*, Hesiod describes the creation of woman, "an evil thing in which all men rejoice in their hearts while embracing their own destruction." Zeus ordered her construction as a punishment for mankind after Prometheus stole fire from the gods. Zeus called his creation Pandora ("All-gifts") after the gods' various contributions: Hephaistos fashioned her out of earth (*gaia*); Athene decked her out in finery and taught her to weave; Aphrodite made her irresistibly attractive; and finally Hermes "wrought within her lies and wily words and a deceitful nature." Since Pandora was the mother of the "deadly race and tribe of women," all humankind subsequently had an "earthy" element, but some Greeks expressed a special connection with their native land in myths of autochthony. One such story is the birth of Erechtheus, ancestor of the Athenians, from the earth.

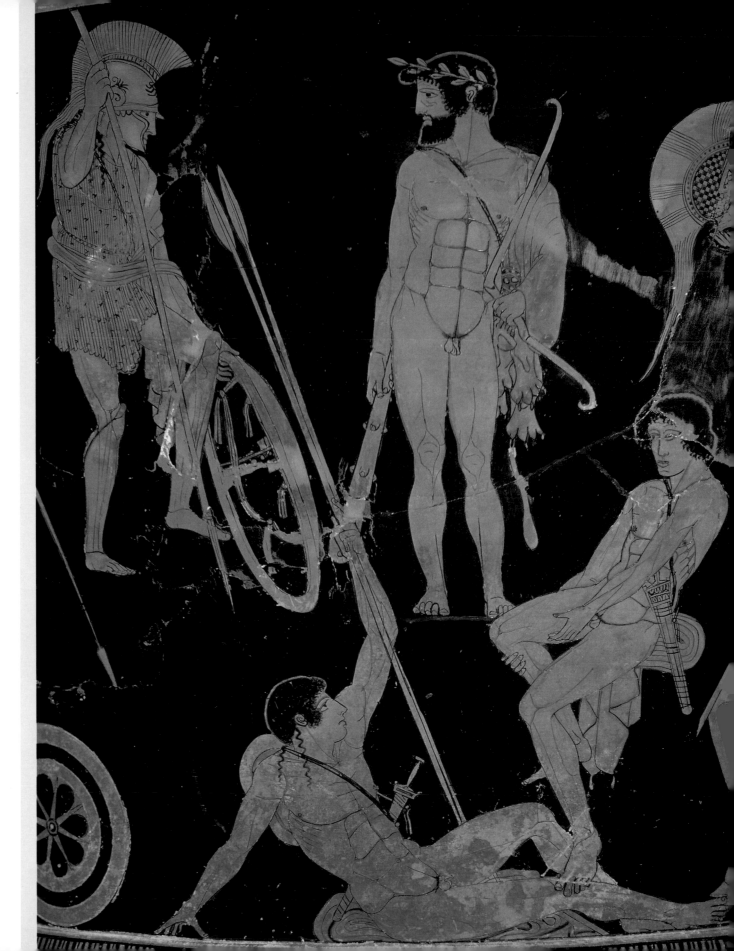

RIGHT: This detail of an Attic red-figure krater by the Niobid Painter, ca. 460 BCE, depicts a whole gathering of heroes. Herakles, in the center, is clearly recognizable by his club, bow, and lionskin, but the others have no distinguishing attributes to aid identification, nor are there any name labels.

FROM ACHILLES TO ALEXANDER:
THE HEROIC IDEAL

Some of Hesiod's race of heroes were "demi-gods," as he called them (meaning that they were of mixed divine and mortal parentage), but many more were simply born to noble families. All were great warriors, however, and ordinary Greeks aspired to the ideal that the heroes represented of *arete*—literally "manliness," but more broadly "virtue," "excellence," and "courage."

Homer's *Iliad* played an important part in shaping the image of the warrior-hero, presenting as it does not only the conflict between the leaders of the Greek cities and a worthy enemy in the form of the noble Trojans, but also the great clash of heroic personalities between Agamemnon, nominal leader of the Greeks, and Achilles, "the best of the Achaeans." Achilles is semi-divine, born of the mortal Peleus and the sea-nymph Thetis, but Thetis' attempts to render him immortal have failed and he is fated either to live a long but obscure life at home, or to die young at Troy with everlasting glory (*kleos*). The terrible "wrath of Achilles," which is the *Iliad*'s stated subject, is caused by Agamemnon having taken away the hero's war-prize, Briseis, a great insult to Achilles' honor. Larger-than-life in all things, Achilles steadfastly refuses to rejoin the fighting, despite all offers of compensation, until he is finally roused by the death of his beloved companion Patroklos at Hektor's hands. Stricken with grief, he rampages across the battlefield, slaughtering Trojans "as furious fire rages through the deep valleys of a dry mountain, and the deep forest burns," until he finally avenges Patroklos by killing Hektor.

RIGHT: In 1972 two bronze statues—one of which is shown here—were found in the sea near Riace, southern Italy. Both perfectly embody the warrior ideal. Dating from ca. 460–450 BCE, each stands around 6 feet, 6 inches (2 m) tall. The reflective surface of the bronze shows off the rippling musculature of the statues' heroic nudity; their lips and nipples are copper, their teeth silver, and their eyes are inlaid.

Other characters in the *Iliad* act as a foil to Achilles' rather excessive brand of heroism. The Trojan leader Hektor, for example, is sympathetically portrayed as a family man much loved by his people, although still a formidable warrior, as is his second-in-command Aeneas. Decidedly unheroic is the Trojan prince Paris, who started the war by breaching all the laws of respect and hospitality when he abducted his host Menelaos' wife Helen from Sparta. Paris is described as beautiful but lacking strength and courage, and his weapon is the coward's bow, with which, ironically, he eventually kills the great Achilles.

The Homeric heroes remained the ultimate warrior role models throughout antiquity, and many were actively worshiped in the states in which they were

BELOW: Second only to Achilles among the Greek heroes at Troy was Ajax. On this Attic red-figure cup of ca. 490 BCE he is seen, to the left, being urged on by Athene as he overcomes Hektor, to whose assistance Artemis is rushing. Just to the right of Ajax's shield is a rock, which the *Iliad* describes Ajax as throwing at Hektor to knock him off his feet.

supposedly born—there was a sanctuary of Menelaos at Sparta, and the people of Salamis performed rituals for Ajax—but there were also some historical embodiments of the heroic ideal. The Spartans in general had a reputation for military prowess and courageous refusal to surrender, summed up in the collection of *Spartan Sayings* preserved among the works of Plutarch. These sayings included a Spartan woman's injunction to her son, about to set off to war, to "come back with your shield or on it"—in other words, return either victorious or dead. The absolute epitome of Spartan bravery, however, was the famous last stand made by King Leonidas and his three hundred companions when they defended the pass at Thermopylae against the Persians in 480 BCE: "Here they defended themselves with swords, if they happened still to have them, and with their hands and teeth, until the barbarians overwhelmed them ...." (Herodotus). Some forty years later what were supposedly Leonidas' remains were brought back to Sparta and a cult was instituted in his honor. During the Peloponnesian War, the Spartan general Brasidas was also given heroic honors after his death, not in his home town but at Amphipolis, the city he had "liberated" from Athenian domination.

For the Athenians, the high point of patriotic bravery was marked by the battle of Marathon in 490 BCE, at which the Athenians were led by Miltiades. It is still possible to visit the enormous tumulus that is the tomb of the 192 Athenians who died at Marathon—all were given the exceptional privilege of being buried on the battlefield because "their *arete*

LEFT: Traditionally known as "Leonidas," this figure of a hoplite soldier was found on the Spartan akropolis. It is made of marble imported from Paros, and has been dated, on stylistic grounds, to the first quarter of the 5th century BCE.

was considered to be outstanding" (Thucydides). Also held in high esteem were the so-called Tyrannicides, Harmodios and Aristogeiton, who assassinated Peisistratos' son Hipparchos in 514 BCE. Their act did not, in fact, end the Peisistratid tyranny, which continued for a few more years under Hippias, and Kleisthenes' reforms (see pages 28–9) were in practice a great deal more significant for the development of democracy, but it was symbolically powerful. The descendants of the Tyrannicides were granted free meals at state expense in perpetuity, and a statue of the pair was erected in the Athenian Agora. When this piece was looted by the Persians in 480–479 BCE it was immediately replaced with a new statue, which was much copied by later admirers of the democratic ideal.

In the fourth century BCE, the Macedonian Alexander the Great, a charismatic military leader himself, took a special interest in the heroes of myth. His family claimed descent from Herakles—a hundred years earlier Alexander I had appealed to this lineage in defense of his Greek nationality and consequent right to participate in the Olympic Games. Alexander the Great had himself represented on coins wearing the hero's trademark lionskin, dedicated altars to him, and even gave the name "Herakles" to his illegitimate son by Barsine, daughter of the Persian satrap Artabazos. According to various accounts of his life, Alexander took his annotated copy of the *Iliad* with him on campaign, and when he first crossed into Asia Minor he paid his respects at Troy, where he poured libations to the heroes of the Greek army. He is supposed to have run a race beside the stele that marked the grave of Achilles, and remarked on Achilles' good fortune in having had such a great poet as Homer render his deeds immortal.

BELOW: The heroic theme of this Hellenistic ivory relief is entirely appropriate for a decorative chape (the end of a scabbard): two Greeks, possibly a warrior and a boy, battle an Amazon on horseback.

MANY-TOWERED TROY

The story of the Trojan War extends well beyond the few days recounted in the *Iliad*. The events leading up to the conflict, the early years of the siege, the actual destruction of Troy, and the Greek heroes' various returns home were recounted in other poems of the "Epic Cycle," and later provided much material for Attic tragedy. The tale begins when the goddess Eris ("strife" personified) throws into a wedding crowd an apple inscribed "For the fairest," a title hotly contested by Hera, Athene, and Aphrodite. Zeus delegates the task of adjudication to the Trojan prince Paris; Aphrodite then promises him the most beautiful woman in the world—Helen, wife of Menelaos—and thereby wins the contest. When he abducts Helen from Sparta, Paris inadvertently activates a vow taken by all of the young Helen's suitors, who had agreed to come to the assistance of whichever man should win her hand in marriage. In mustering the Greek princes, Menelaos is helped by his brother Agamemnon, who becomes the leader of the expedition against Troy.

The Greeks spend ten years encamped outside the walls of "many-towered Troy," as Homer calls it; the *Iliad* is set in the final year of the siege. After the death of the Trojan leader Hektor, and a brief truce for his burial, war resumes, with a number of allies coming to the Trojans' aid: Achilles slays both the Amazon queen Penthesileia and the Ethiopian prince Memnon, son of Eos, but then he himself is killed by Paris and Apollo. The Greeks enlist the help of Achilles' son Neoptolemos, and Philoktetes, who has the mighty bow once owned by Herakles, but Troy only falls in the end because of the trick of the Wooden Horse (see illustration, right). In the course of the sack, Hektor's son Astyanax is flung to his death from the city walls. Only the Trojan hero Aeneas, son of Aphrodite, and one or two companions escape, but the Greeks too suffer heavy losses, and few of them return home unscathed.

OPPOSITE: **A rare surviving Greek representation of the Wooden Horse—hidden in which the Greeks finally managed to gain entry into Troy—is this clay** *pithos* **(storage jar) from Mykonos, which was made ca. 670 BCE, not very long after the composition of the** *Odyssey*. **This detail depicts some of the Greek warriors still inside the wheeled horse, looking out through little windows and handing armor down to those who are already outside.**

THE WANDERINGS OF ODYSSEUS

The longest journey home after the Trojan War was that of the "resourceful" Odysseus, as recounted in the *Odyssey*. Having left Troy with 12 ships, Odysseus almost immediately begins to lose men, first at the city of the Kikones, then in the land of the lotus-eaters. In the cave of the Cyclopes Polyphemos several men are eaten before Odysseus makes their captor drunk and blinds him with a red-hot stake, announcing his identity as "Nobody"; Polyphemos cries out that "Nobody" is killing him, so no help comes, and the following morning Odysseus and his companions escape. As they sail away, Odysseus rashly calls out his real name, bringing the wrath of Polyphemos' father Poseidon upon his head.

Next the group visits the island of Aiolos, keeper of the winds, who sends them on their way with the storm winds tied up in a bag. When they are within sight of Ithaca, the hero's home, Odysseus' men open what they think is a bag of treasure, and they are driven back to Aiolos, who refuses to help a second time. Sailing on they come to the land of the Laistrygonians, savage man-eaters who bombard the ships with rocks and harpoon the men like fish; only Odysseus' own ship escapes.

This much-reduced party reaches the island of Circe, who customarily turns visitors into animals, but Odysseus counters her magic and spends a year making love to her while his men enjoy unlimited food and wine. Eventually they decide to continue their journey, but first they must visit the Underworld to seek advice from the seer Teiresias. After this they safely negotiate the Sirens—monsters whose irresistible singing lures sailors into their murderous clutches (see illustration, right)—but in steering clear of the

BELOW: This unusual black-figure *skyphos* of ca. 400 BCE is Boiotian, from the sanctuary of the Kabeiroi at Thebes. Comic versions of Odysseus' adventures feature on both sides: here he is crossing the sea on a raft improvised from two amphorae, while Boreas (the north wind) blows from the right; on the reverse he is shown meeting Circe for the first time.

whirlpool Charybdis they lose several men to the six-headed sea-monster Scylla. On the island of Thrinakia the remaining men kill some of the sun god Helios' cattle, for which sacrilege Zeus sends a violent storm, breaking up the ship and leaving only Odysseus himself alive. Odysseus is duly washed up on the island of Ogygia, where the goddess Calypso keeps him as her lover for seven years, until the gods compel her to release him. Odysseus sets sail on a raft, which is once again shipwrecked by Poseidon, but this time he swims ashore on Phaiakia. The Phaiakians deliver Odysseus back to Ithaca, where, disguised as a beggar, he infiltrates his own palace, which has been occupied by the many suitors who hope to marry his wife Penelope and become king. Having proved his identity by stringing the great bow, Odysseus kills the suitors with the help of his son Telemachos and the faithful swineherd Eumaios, before being reunited with the long-suffering Penelope.

BELOW: This Attic red-figure *stamnos* dated ca. 450 BCE shows Odysseus' encounter with the Sirens—half-bird, half-woman creatures. Two of the Sirens are perched on the cliffs to either side while a third may be swooping down for a closer inspection or plummeting to her death in frustration. The ship's crew continue rowing undistracted, their ears safely blocked with wax, while Odysseus is bound to the mast so that he can hear but will not be able to succumb to the Sirens' seductive song.

IN THE WAKE OF ODYSSEUS

The Ionian island of Ithaca (right), just off the west coast of mainland Greece, has been identified with Odysseus' home since antiquity. Although some scholars have argued in favor of nearby Leukas, Ithaca does seem a fair match for Homer's description of it in the *Odyssey*: "It is rugged and not fit for driving horses, and yet, although narrow, it is not altogether poor. It provides plentiful corn and wine; it always has rain and fresh dew. It has good pasture for goats and cattle; there is wood of every kind, and never-failing watering-places are there." The neighboring island of Kephalonia is sometimes identified with the utopian land of the Phaiakians, Odysseus' last port of call, where he met the princess Nausikaa and the king Alkinoos, and told the story of his wanderings at the feast held in his honor.

The account of Odysseus' subsequent home-coming provides more physical description of Ithaca: " … there is a bay named Phorkys, after the old man of the sea, where two steep headlands jut out, crouching before the bay, which protect it from the storm-winds' great waves outside; but inside, well-decked ships can ride without mooring when they reach its anchorage. At the head of the bay is a long-leaved olive-tree, and near it a pleasantly shady cave, sacred to the nymphs, who are called Naides …." It is tempting to identify this spot with the "Cave of the Nymphs" excavated at Polis Bay, to the north of the island, where finds included the remains of a dozen magnificent geometric-period tripods, reminiscent of the rich gifts Odysseus brought home from Phaiakia. There is another traditional candidate for the cave at Dhexia Bay, at the south end of the island.

THE LABORS OF HERAKLES

B est known of all Greek heroes is Herakles. Hundreds of monster-slaying exploits were attributed to him, but the idea of the 12 labors has proved the most enduring. These were imposed on him by his cousin Eurystheus, king of Tiryns, usually by way of expiation for Herakles' murder of his own family in a fit of madness.

First Herakles had to kill the Nemean Lion, which he choked to death because its hide was invulnerable; ever afterward he wore this lionskin as both trophy and protection. Next he tackled the Lernaean hydra, a many-headed water-monster that grew two heads for every one chopped off. The next task entailed capturing the golden-horned Kerynian hind, which was sacred to Artemis, and bringing it back to Tiryns alive. Similarly, the fierce Erymanthian boar, which had been terrorizing Arkadia, was delivered alive to Eurystheus, who was so scared that he hid in a great

RIGHT: **All 12 of Herakles' labors are depicted on the metopes of the temple of Zeus at Olympia, ca. 460 BCE. On this one, Herakles has a cushion on his shoulders as he supports the weight of the Heavens, with a little effortless assistance from Athene. He is approached by Atlas, who holds out the apples brought back from the garden of the Hesperides (see also illustration, opposite).**

bronze jar. Herakles displayed more skill than brute force in the fifth labor, which was to clean out the cattle-stables of Augeias, king of Elis; he achieved this by diverting Olympia's two rivers, the Alpheios and Peneios, to sweep away the dung. Killing the birds that were infesting the Arkadian lake Stymphalos also involved some cunning—Herakles scared them from their coverts with a rattle before shooting them with his arrows.

The first six tasks were all set in the Peloponnese, but the remaining six took Herakles steadily farther afield. He captured the Cretan bull and tamed the man- eating mares of the Thracian king Diomedes by feeding their master to them. He traveled to the Black Sea to fetch the belt of the Amazon queen Hippolyte, and then to the far west to capture the cattle of Geryon, who lived beyond the bounds of Ocean. The garden of the Hesperides was also situated in the distant west, beyond the sunset and near the place where Atlas held up the Heavens; Herakles either fetched the Hesperides' golden apples himself, having slain the guardian serpent Ladon, or sent Atlas to do the task for him. Finally, Herakles descended to the Underworld where Hades agreed to let him take Kerberos (see page 60) up to the Earth provided he did so without weapons; having been shown to Eurystheus, the hound was quickly returned.

After many more adventures Herakles eventually died a terrible death, poisoned by the blood of the centaur Nessos, but his sufferings on Earth were rewarded: the gods welcomed him to Olympos (see illustration, page 8), where he feasts among the immortals "untroubled and unaging all his days" (Hesiod).

THESEUS: THE STATESMAN HERO

Unlike the Panhellenic Herakles, Theseus, whose story is told at length by Plutarch, was especially associated with Athens. He was son of Aigeus, an early king of Athens, as a result of a brief liaison Aigeus enjoyed with the princess Aithra at Troizen in the Argolid when he was visiting her father Pittheus on his return from Delphi. Some said, however, that Theseus was the son of Poseidon, who had also slept with Aithra that night. When he was old enough, Theseus immediately proved his worth by lifting a great rock under which Aigeus had left sandals and a sword as tokens by which the boy might be recognized if he came to Athens. Rather than take the easy sea-crossing from Troizen, Theseus determined to take the land route to Attica around the Saronic Gulf, encountering various villains on his journey. He gave each of these a taste of his own medicine, such as Skiron, who compelled travelers to wash his feet, then kicked them over the cliffs into the sea to be eaten by a monstrous turtle, and Prokrustes, who would offer travelers a bed for the night and then stretch or cut his guests to size.

When Theseus arrived in Athens, Aigeus did not at first recognize him, but the young man proved himself yet again by capturing the Marathonian bull. Shortly afterward the tribute became due for Minos, king of Crete, of seven youths and seven girls who would be fed to the Minotaur. Theseus went with them, and succeeded not only in killing the Minotaur, but also in finding his way back out of the Labyrinth, by means of a ball of thread given to him by Minos' daughter Ariadne. The couple sailed away together, but Theseus soon abandoned Ariadne, either on the gods' orders or because he had fallen in love with another girl. He sailed on to Delos, where he made offerings of thanks to Apollo, before returning to Athens. Theseus had promised his father that he would change the black sail of his ship to white (or scarlet) if he was bearing good news, but he forgot, and the despairing Aigeus jumped off the Akropolis to his death; the Aegean Sea was named after him.

Theseus thus became king of Athens, after which he had various other adventures, but many of the deeds attributed to his mature years are obviously projections of historical political events. He was supposed to have gathered together the Attic villages into a single state of Athens, to have founded the Panathenaia festival and the Isthmian Games, and even to have voluntarily handed over power to the people. This made him the first hero of Athenian democracy, and he was worshiped at Athens with an annual festival and monthly sacrifices.

BELOW: The Minotaur, a man with the head and tail of a bull, was the monstrous offspring of Pasiphae and the bull sent by Poseidon. On this Attic black-figure amphora, made ca. 550 BCE, Theseus cuts the Minotaur's throat, from which blood pours forth dramatically. The killing is watched by Ariadne (behind Theseus) and others.

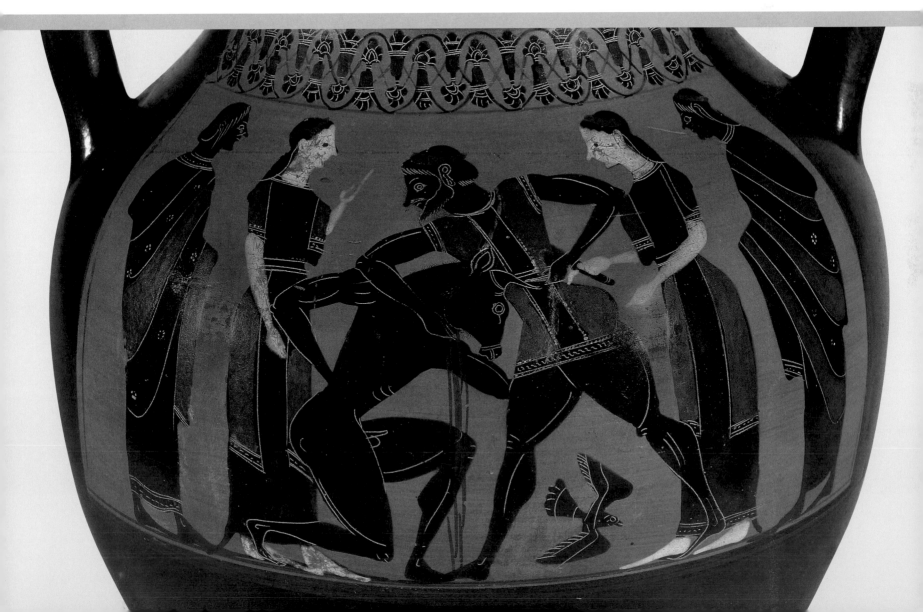

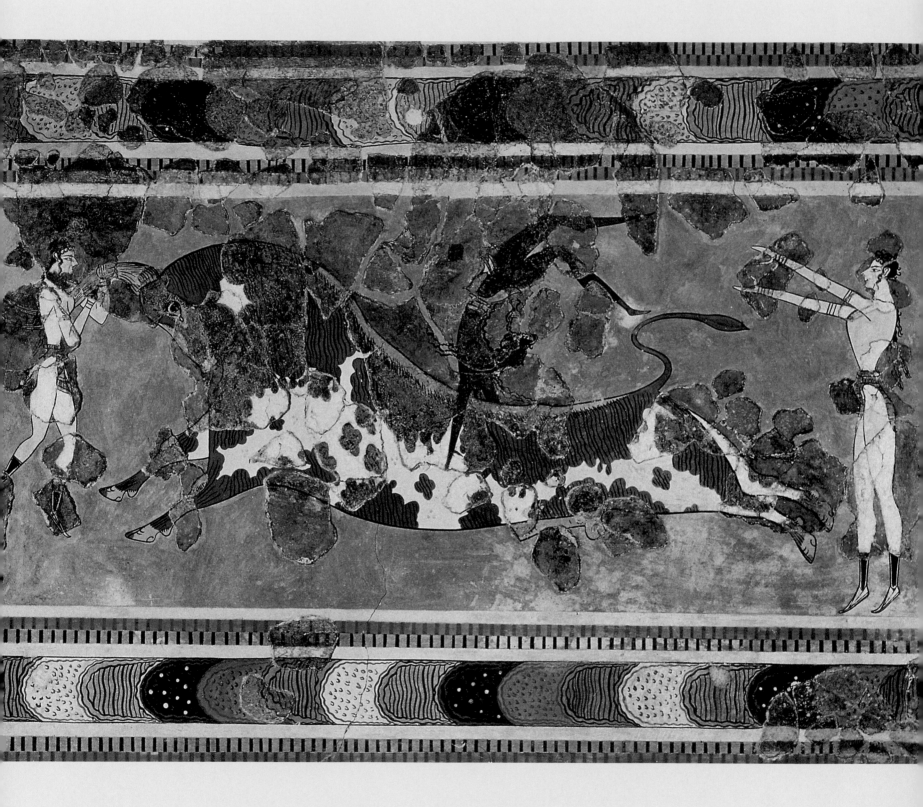

LEAPING THE BULL

There has been much speculation about the origins of the story of Theseus and the Minotaur. The myth was obviously popular on Crete in the Roman imperial period, when several coin types from Knossos show a labyrinth, and one even has the bull-headed monster on the reverse. The Minoan palace excavated at Knossos (see pages 10–11) is indeed very complex architecturally, and could have appeared "labyrinthine" to a visitor. There are also plenty of bull images among the finds, such as this beautiful bull's-head drinking vessel made of serpentine, limestone, rock crystal, and gold (above). The wall paintings of the palace include a scene of bull-leaping (opposite), in which one figure grasps the bull's horns while another somersaults over its back, and a third stands ready to catch him.

THE QUEST FOR THE GOLDEN FLEECE

BELOW: **Inside this Attic red-figure cup by Douris, ca. 470 BCE, a magnificent dragon has actually swallowed Jason (his name is inscribed between his dangling arms and hair). Athene, holding an owl in her hand and with both helmet and aegis beautifully decorated, is perhaps ensuring that the serpent-like dragon disgorges its prey. In the background the golden fleece hangs in a tree.**

M any Greek heroes took part in the voyage led by Jason in search of the golden fleece. The story is alluded to in the *Odyssey*, but it is known to us in detail from Apollonius of Rhodes' Hellenistic epic the *Argonautika*. The golden fleece was that of the miraculous talking, flying ram that had rescued Phrixos and Helle from their wicked stepmother's plots: the girl fell off en route, giving her name to the Hellespont, but Phrixos was carried safely to Aia in Colchis, where he sacrificed the ram to Zeus and gave the fleece to king Aietes, son of Helios. Aietes hung it in an oak tree in a grove sacred to Ares, where it was guarded by a dragon that never slept.

RIGHT: **This Attic red-figure krater made ca. 400 BCE depicts the death of the giant Talos, who tried to prevent the Argonauts from landing on Crete. Talos' only weak spot was his ankle, where a bronze nail sealed in the divine ichor that ran through his veins, but here he is depicted succumbing to the magical powers of Medea, who stands to the far left in oriental dress with her box of potions. Talos (painted a yellowy white to indicate his bronze skin) is beginning to fall into the arms of Castor and Pollux (recognizable by their horses), who were among the Argonauts. To the right, the marine setting is indicated by the presence of Poseidon, with his trident, and Amphitrite.**

Pelias had usurped the throne of Iolkos in Thessaly, to which his half-brother Jason was the rightful heir, so he set Jason the seemingly impossible task of fetching the fleece. Jason, however, had the support of Hera, whom Pelias had offended; Athene advised on the construction of Jason's ship the *Argo*, and fifty of the bravest heroes in Greece responded to the call to join the expedition.

The Argonauts had many adventures on their way to Colchis, including their memorable encounter with the women of Lemnos, who had earlier massacred all their menfolk and needed to conceive children to repopulate the island. In Thrace Jason and his followers rescued the blind seer Phineus from the Harpies who kept stealing his food. The Argonauts safely negotiated the Clashing Rocks at the northern end of the Bosphoros, and eventually reached Aia, where Aietes agreed to hand over the fleece if Jason could perform a series of tasks. Hera caused the king's daughter Medea to fall in love with Jason, and with the help of her magic salve of invulnerability he succeeded in yoking the fire-breathing bulls, and killing the army of men sprung from dragon's teeth sewn in the ground. Knowing that Aietes would not keep his word, Medea used her powers to put the dragon to sleep while Jason stole the golden fleece, before escaping with it on the *Argo*.

The return journey, too, was eventful, including encounters with some of the hazards that would later be met by Odysseus, and with Talos, the bronze man who guarded Crete (see illustration, above). When they reached Iolkos, Medea tricked Pelias' daughters into killing him: thinking they were rejuvenating him, they cut their father into pieces and boiled him in a pot. He was succeeded by his son Akastos, while Jason and Medea fled to Corinth, where, according to some, Jason was eventually crushed to death by a beam from the *Argo*.

PERSEUS AND THE GORGON'S HEAD

Like Jason, Perseus was initially cheated of his kingdom and sent on an "impossible" quest. His mother Danae had been imprisoned in a bronze chamber by her father Akrisios, king of Argos, after the oracle said he would be killed by a son of hers. She nonetheless became pregnant by Zeus, but when Perseus was born Akrisios shut up mother and baby in a chest and cast it into the sea. They came ashore on Seriphos, where they were taken in by Diktys, brother of the island's king Polydektes, and lived happily until Polydektes decided he wanted to marry Danae. Perseus was sent to fetch the head of the Gorgon Medusa to keep him out of the way.

In his mission Perseus had the help of both Athene and Hermes, who sent him first to the three Graiai ("Old Women"). Perseus forced them to reveal the whereabouts of certain nymphs, who duly gave him various magical items that add a folktale element to the story. Perseus flew on his new winged sandals beyond Ocean to the land of the Gorgons, whom he found asleep. Because anyone who looked at them directly would be turned to stone, he used the reflection in Athene's shield as a guide, and with the *harpe* (curved dagger) supplied by Hermes he cut off Medusa's head. From Medusa's severed neck sprang the winged horse Pegasos and the warrior Chrysaor—Medusa's two immortal sisters, Stheno and Euryale, gave chase to Perseus, but he escaped with the help of Hades' cap of darkness.

On his way home Perseus came to the land of the Ethiopians, where the princess Andromeda was about to be devoured by a sea monster, sent by Poseidon to punish the boasting of her mother Kassiopeia. King Kepheus agreed that Perseus could marry Andromeda if he could kill the monster, which he duly did; Kepheus' brother, who had been betrothed to Andromeda, tried to stop her marrying Perseus, but was soon turned to stone. The same fate befell Polydektes when

LEFT: **On this south-Italian amphora of unusual type, ca. 340 BCE and attributed to the Metope Group, Perseus battles with a sea-monster, ridden by Eros, whose presence indicates the romantic outcome. Perseus' winged boots and the *harpe* can clearly be seen. Above, Andromeda stands chained to a rock; Kepheus (with white beard and staff) and the other men are marked out as "barbarians" by their Persian-style caps.**

Perseus reached Seriphos and found that he was persecuting Danae. Having made Diktys king, Perseus gave his magic gifts back to Hermes and handed over Medusa's head to Athene, who ever afterward wore it on her aegis.

Perseus eventually returned to the Greek mainland, where he accidentally killed his grandfather Akrisios with a discus, thus fulfilling the oracle. He was too ashamed to take his rightful place on the throne of Argos, but exchanged Argos for Mycenae (see pages 16–17), where he founded the dynasty that a few generations later would produce Herakles.

ABOVE: **Perseus, with winged boots, flees from Medusa's Gorgon sisters toward his waiting chariot. This is a detail from an Attic black-figure** *dinos* **(wine-mixing bowl) of ca. 600 BCE.**

BEASTS AND MONSTERS

The celebrated heroes Herakles, Theseus, Jason, and Perseus all demonstrated their physical prowess and cunning by vanquishing monsters, of which a great variety appear in Greek myth. In the *Theogony*, Hesiod describes a whole family of monstrous beings descended from the ancient sea deities Keto and Phorkys, the offspring of Earth and Pontos (Sea). Keto bore the Graiai and the Gorgons (see pages 102–103), then Echidna, who was "half quick-glancing, fair-cheeked nymph, and half again a monstrous snake, huge and terrible, writhing and raw-flesh-eating down in the depths of the sacred earth." Echidna's offspring included several of the beasts overcome by Herakles: the multi-headed hounds Kerberos and Geryon's guard-dog Orthos, the Nemean lion, and the Lernaean hydra. The three-headed Geryon was the grandson of Medusa via Chrysaor. Geryon's monstrous form posed a particular

BELOW: **This unusual gold fibula (brooch), which was produced in the late 5th century BCE, is decorated with images of a griffin and a sea horse.**

---104---

challenge to Greek artists who depicted him variously with one or three torsos, up to six arms, and two or six legs.

Fabulous hybrid beasts became popular in Greek art of the archaic period under the influence of stories and images from the east. Some of the earliest clay or bronze animal figurines buried with the dead or dedicated at sanctuaries were Centaurs (half-man, half-horse) and the griffins that once decorated great bronze tripod-cauldrons (see illustration, page 18). Griffins had an eagle's head and wings but the body of a lion, and were supposed to live at the northern limits of the world, where they guarded hordes of gold against the one-eyed Arimaspians. In the Roman imperial period the griffin becomes associated with Nemesis ("Retribution"), sharing her relentless pursuit of vengeance. Also part-lion was the Chimaira, another offspring of Echidna, which Apollodoros describes: "it had the foreparts of a lion, the tail of a serpent, and a third head in the middle of a goat, through which it breathed fire … one creature, it had the power of three beasts." The Corinthian hero Bellerophon was set the task of killing this monster by Iobates, king of Lykia, which he succeeded in doing with the help of his winged horse Pegasos, offspring of Medusa.

Many Greek monsters were female in gender, including several that were half-woman in form. Both the Sirens (see pages 90–91) and the Harpies (see page 101) were often represented as birds with women's heads, while yet another of Echidna's children was the Sphinx, a winged lion with a woman's head, inspired by the sphinxes of Egypt and the Near East. In myth she is best known for terrorizing the people of Thebes, devouring anyone who gave the wrong answer to her riddle, until Oedipus came up with the solution (see page 109). More generally, though, the image of the sphinx was carved on tombstones, where it was believed she would guard the dead from disturbance.

ABOVE: Potters sometimes demonstrated their skill by making vases in unusual forms. This late 5th-century BCE *lekythos* from the Bosphoros region is in the shape of a sphinx, her femininity emphasized by the bare breasts and elaborate gilded hair and jewelry.

SNAKES AND DRAGONS

Creatures of the depths of earth and sea, snakes and water-serpents (Greek *drakones*),
had both positive and negative associations for the Greeks. Asklepios, god of healing, and his
daughter Health were always accompanied by snakes, which had links with agricultural
fertility in the cult of Demeter. A serpent-like dragon guarded the golden fleece (see pages
100–101) and the apples of the Hesperides, and the snakes of Athene's aegis had a similarly
protective function. Medusa's hair was often depicted as consisting of snakes, as here on this
early 5th-century BCE bronze mirror from southern Italy (above). More actively malevolent
was the Lernaean hydra killed by Herakles, and the water-serpents that killed the Trojan
priest Laokoon and his sons, as portrayed in a famous Hellenistic statue-group (opposite).

FATE, VENGEANCE, AND THE TRAGIC HERO

Many of the heroes celebrated by Homer and Hesiod had their stories reshaped in fifth-century BCE Athens for the tragic stage. Aeschylus' *Oresteia* trilogy, produced in 458 BCE, elaborates the tale of the return home from Troy of Agamemnon, leader of the Greeks, and the bloody events that followed. In the first play, Agamemnon's wife Klytaimnestra murders him in the bath. In the *Libation Bearers*, the royal couple's son Orestes returns from exile and avenges his dead father by

slaying both his mother and her lover Aigisthos. The final part of Aeschylus' trilogy is the *Eumenides*, the "Kindly Ones," a euphemism for the Furies who pursue Orestes for having spilt his mother's blood. He seeks purification at Delphi, whence Apollo sends him to Athens to be tried at the homicide court of the Areopagos; when there is a hung jury Athene gives the casting vote in Orestes' favor. Thus the cycle of vengeance called for by the ancient aristocratic code of honor is finally broken by the intervention of the modern, democratic institution of the law court.

The enlightened city of Athens is also made to offer sanctuary to Oedipus in Sophocles' *Oedipus at Kolonos*, but the main events of the hero's terrible story are related in *Oedipus the King*. The myth is a parable of the inevitability of fate: believing himself to be the child of the king and queen of Corinth, Oedipus flees to avoid the oracle's prediction that he will kill his father and marry his mother. He travels to Thebes, where he marries the recently bereaved queen Jokasta, unaware that her dead husband Laios was the very man Oedipus had just killed in a roadside brawl. Thus Oedipus fulfills the oracle, because he is really a prince of Thebes, exposed at birth but rescued and removed to Corinth by shepherds. Sophocles' treatment of the story, however, shifts the focus by starting when Oedipus is already king of Thebes, respected for having solved the Sphinx's riddle, and with children by Jokasta. The play centers on Oedipus' determination to root out the cause of the plague that is afflicting his people, which the oracle tells him is the pollution arising from the unpunished murder of Laios. Oedipus relentlessly uncovers the truth, and thus brings about the delayed realization of his own downfall. Oedipus finally asserts his own will by blinding himself and retreating into self-imposed exile.

BELOW: "What goes on four legs in the morning, then two legs, then three?" This is the riddle of the Sphinx, which Oedipus is puzzling over in this detail from a south-Italian volute-krater dated ca. 340–330 BCE. The answer is "man," who crawls as a baby, walks upright in his prime, and hobbles with a stick in old age.

TALES OF TRANSGRESSION

Alongside the tales of warrior prowess and heroic honor, Greek myth has a number of stories that demonstrate the other end of the spectrum: types of behavior that were liable to divine punishment. A major area of transgression involved offenses against various goddesses' modesty. When Teiresias saw Athene bathing naked, for example, she struck him blind, but gave him some compensation in the form of prophetic powers (see page 56 for a different version of the story). Another frequent kind of transgression was the challenge to a deity's area of

RIGHT: When Ixion attempted to rape Hera, Zeus tricked him into sleeping with a cloud fashioned in Hera's form. The impregnated cloud gave birth to Kentauros, father of the race of Centaurs, but Ixion boasted of his conquest, so Zeus tied him to an ever-turning wheel for his presumption. Ixion's wheel nicely fits the circular tondo-space of this south-Italian cup of ca. 400 BCE, although there is no indication of his bonds.

prowess, such as Niobe boasting about her children (see page 74). Arachne presumptuously challenged Athene to a weaving contest, as a result of which she was transformed into a spider. The Thracian bard Thamyris also suffered a terrible fate for challenging the Muses to a singing competition: the goddesses agreed that he could sleep with each of them in turn if he won, but when he lost they struck him blind and took away his musical skills. Worse still was the Phrygian satyr Marsyas' punishment for daring to compete with his pipes against Apollo's lyre-playing: he was hung on a pine tree and flayed alive.

Various other transgressors endured eternal punishments in the Underworld. The site of Ixion's wheel was usually said to be Tartaros, where the giant Tityos, who had tried to rape Leto, could also be found, sprawled over two acres of ground with two vultures tearing at his constantly regenerating liver. On his visit to the Underworld, Odysseus saw Tantalos, father of Niobe, who had once been a favorite of the gods, but offended them by serving up his own son Pelops in a stew to test their omniscience, or by stealing some of the gods' ambrosia and nectar. His punishment was to stand forever up to his neck in water, which would drain away every time he bent to drink, and to be surrounded by branches laden with fruit, which blew out of reach whenever he tried to pick them. The *Odyssey* also describes the fate of Sisyphos, who had incurred the gods' anger by a whole series of offenses, including informing on Zeus when he had carried off the river-god Asopos' daughter Aigina, and cheating death by tying up Thanatos himself. To keep him out of further mischief, Sisyphos was condemned always to push uphill a great rock, which rolled back down again every time he reached the top.

ABOVE: **Aktaion's death is graphically depicted on this late 4th-century BCE south-Italian *skyphos* (deep drinking cup). The horns indicate the beginnings of his transformation into a stag, as he tries in vain to defend himself against the hounds that are tearing at his legs and shoulders. His struggles are watched by a small figure of Pan, the pastoral god who is half-goat, half-man.**

TALES OF TRANSFORMATION

O ne form of punishment for transgressive mortals was transformation, but such metamorphosis could serve a variety of purposes. In some cases it saved a mortal from a worse fate, as when the river-god Peneios turned his daughter Daphne into a laurel tree so that she might escape Apollo's unwelcome embraces. Zeus tried to protect his beloved Io from Hera's jealousy by turning her into a cow, but his suspicious wife asked for the cow as a gift and set the Hundred-Eyed Argos to watch her. When Hermes rescued Io by killing Argos, Hera sent a gadfly to drive her rival wandering all over the Earth, but eventually Io reached Egypt where she was restored to human form, and later identified with the Egyptian goddess Isis. Another victim of Hera's spite was Kallisto, a companion of Artemis until she was raped by Zeus, her unchastity discovered when she undressed to bathe. When Kallisto gave birth to a son, Arkas, Hera was so incensed that she turned the girl into a bear, in which form she wandered the woods for many years. Arkas grew up to be a huntsman, and was unwittingly about to kill his mother when Zeus finally took notice of her plight and caught up both mother and son into the Heavens, where they became the constellation Ursa Major (the "Great Bear") and the bright star Arcturus ("Bear-Guardian").

The mirror image of such immortalization among the stars was the Olympian gods' habit of adopting human and animal disguises. Zeus is especially well known for his many amorous disguises (see page 54), but deities might take on human forms in order to deliver messages or go unobserved among mortals for all kinds of

BELOW: **This Hellenistic figurine from Tanagra, Boiotia, depicts Zeus' abduction of the Phoenician princess Europa. In the form of a bull he carried her over the sea to Crete, where she gave birth to Minos, Rhadamanthys, and Sarpedon. When he had finished with the disguise, Zeus set the bull shape among the stars as the constellation Taurus.**

reasons. A particular gift for shape-shifting, though, seems to have belonged to sea-deities. In the *Odyssey* Menelaos recounts the problems he had catching Proteus, Poseidon's sealherd, in order to obtain his advice: "first he became a well-maned lion, and then a serpent, a panther, and a great boar; he became running water and a high-towering tree …." Herakles had similar difficulties with the sea god Nereus when seeking the way to the garden of the Hesperides. The trick was also used by various sea-nymphs in their, always vain, attempts to shake off unwanted suitors: Thetis went through a whole repertoire of shapes before being caught by Peleus and bearing him Achilles; Psamathe turned herself into a seal (*phoke*) but failed to escape Aiakos, to whom she bore a son called Phokos; and in the epic *Kypria*, Nemesis "sped across the great deep in the form of a fish … she kept turning into such terrible beasts as the land nurtures," but was in the shape of a wild goose when Zeus eventually overtook her, and she laid the egg from which Helen of Troy would be born.

THE LIFE OF THE SPIRIT

Religious observance was of fundamental importance to the ancient Greeks. Ritual expressed the relationship between mortals and the gods; on a daily basis individuals prayed and made small offerings to the deities that presided over the household, while state institutions began the day's proceedings with prayers, libations, and sacrifices. For both men and women, there were rituals to mark every stage of the life-cycle, from birth through coming-of-age and marriage to death. At times of personal crisis it might be necessary to visit a healing shrine or consult a diviner for advice, and many people chose to be initiated into a mystery cult. Every city had its own calendar of festivals, and even smaller communities might have their own religious program.

LEFT: It was customary in Greece to bury grave goods with the dead, usually in the form of drinking vessels, weapons, jewelry, toys, or other personal belongings. Burials of the wealthy and powerful included more spectacular pieces in precious metals, such as this beautiful late 4th-century BCE wreath made of gold with blue and green glass-paste inlays.

RIGHT: This 4th-century BCE bronze in the form of a tragic mask may have been dedicated to Dionysos, god of the theater.

TEMPLES AND SHRINES

Greek places of worship varied from the small household shrine to the full-scale temple and extended sanctuary complex. Shrines shared by the community usually included an altar, at which animal sacrifices—the central ritual of Greek religion—were performed. For the Olympian gods the altar (*bomos*) was a stone construction raised up from the ground, where the animal was sacrificed with its head pulled back so that the throat was pointing heavenward when cut. If the god had a temple (*naos*), the altar was usually placed in front of it, so that worshipers gathered around the sacrifice would be facing the exterior of the building's east end. The simplest form of temple was a single, roofed chamber, but this developed over the archaic period into the more elaborate design with which we are familiar. This consisted of a central chamber with an entrance porch and a rear chamber, the whole surrounded by a colonnade. The central chamber housed a sacred image, a statue that was regarded as especially holy and often closely identified with the deity him- or herself. Ancient wooden statues were particularly revered and often dressed in real clothes, such as the statue of Athene Polias on the Athenian Akropolis (see pages 68–9). Nonetheless communities often spent large sums of money commissioning new statues from the best sculptors of the day, such as the statue of Zeus at Olympia by Pheidias, which became one of the seven wonders of the ancient world. A temple might stand alone or form part of a larger sanctuary (*hieron*, or "sacred place"), usually dedicated to one main deity but encompassing temples and altars to a number of other gods and heroes too.

Shrines to heroes and other chthonic powers usually had a low hearth or pit, where the sacrificial victim's blood could flow directly down into the ground. A hero's shrine might be little more than such a hearth with the sacred area around it

LEFT: **This late-Hellenistic bronze herm of ca. 100–50 BCE represents the god Dionysos wearing a loosely bound turban. The herm originated as a road- and boundary-marker, representing the god Hermes (see page 78), but the form later came to be used for other deities.**

RIGHT: **The Doric temple at Segesta in western Sicily was begun in the 420s BCE, but construction work was interrupted when war broke out with Selinus in 416 and the building was never completed. The columns have been left unfluted, and the walls of the inner chamber are missing. Nonetheless, the remains that stand to this day are impressive, with 36 columns, entablature, and pediments all intact.**

enclosed or marked in some way. Some deities who had a particular association with nature were worshiped in natural locations, at springs or in sacred groves; natural caves were often the site of rituals for the pastoral god Pan. Caves were also suitable for the worship of Underworld deities, such as the Furies at Athens, who had a sacred cave on the slopes of the Areopagos.

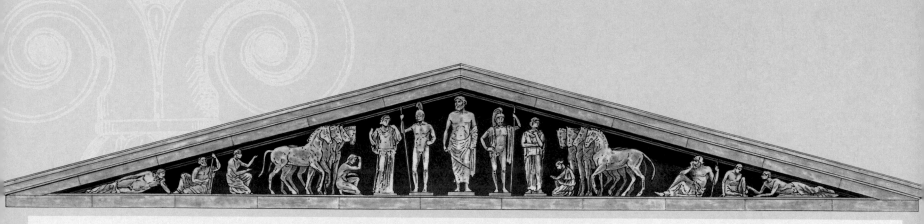

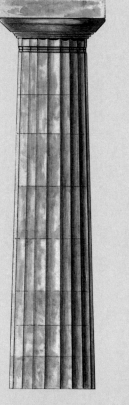

SYMBOLIC ARCHITECTURE

Greek temples combined reverence for the gods with a display of the community's pride and wealth. The Erechtheion on the Athenian Akropolis was part of Perikles' building program (see pages 70–71), although it was not completed until ca. 406 BCE. It owed its highly unusual plan to the number of shrines it incorporated—to Athene Polias and Poseidon, as well as to the hero Erechtheus himself, and Kekrops and his daughter Pandrosos. The female figures used in place of columns in the south porch (opposite) were named "Caryatids" by the Roman writer Vitruvius, after the maidens of Karyai—a Spartan town punished for siding with the Persians during the Persian Wars—but the Erectheion's building accounts refer to them simply as *korai*, "maidens."

The east pediment of the temple of Zeus at Olympia (ca. 470–457 BCE) portrayed a myth of strictly local significance (see illustration, above). The scene captures the tense moment just before the chariot race between Oinomaos, king of Pisa, and Pelops, who is competing for his daughter Hippodameia's hand in marriage; Pelops will win and eventually give his name to the whole Peloponnese.

RITES AND FESTIVALS

The rites performed at temples and shrines of all kinds varied as much as the holy places themselves. Most rituals were accompanied by prayers, for which there were special formulaic phrases, and which might be spoken privately for individual needs, pronounced before a gathering, or spoken in unison by a crowd following the lead of a herald. There was a formulaic element to hymns, too, which often included reference to the deity's life story and sphere of influence. The simplest form of offering was a libation—a few drops of wine or other liquids poured first into a flat dish and then onto the ground, the remainder being drunk by each of those present in turn. Libations might be performed in the home every morning and evening, or at the beginning of a meal, or just before setting off on a journey. Offerings of hair, clothes, or personal belongings were made at rites of passage, particularly in preparation for marriage and in connection with childbirth. More permanent dedications could be made at a sanctuary in the form of votive reliefs, and even statues, representing either the deity or the worshiper.

The heart of Greek religious ritual, however, lay in sacrifice. A few deities demanded "bloodless sacrifices" in the form of the first fruits of cereal and olive crops, of bread, cakes, cooked vegetables, or even burned spices, but most common was the blood sacrifice. The most humble victim would be a dove or cockerel, then a piglet, lamb, or kid, then a full-grown sheep or goat, and at the top end of the

LEFT: The importance of processions is reflected in their frequent depiction in Greek art, most famously on the Parthenon's frieze (see pages 70–71). At the Panathenaia Athene was supposed to receive a "hecatomb," a sacrifice of a hundred oxen. Among the animal victims portrayed on the frieze are a number of heifers, including the one in this detail, which is thought to have inspired Keats' line, "That heifer lowing at the skies ... " (*Ode on a Grecian Urn*).

scale, the ox. To sacrifice to the Olympians was to "fumigate," because the gods were thought to enjoy the smell of the fatty smoke rising, but to a hero one had to "devote" the victim by burning it whole. An individual or family would probably sacrifice one small animal, but the great city festivals in honor of the gods, which usually lasted several days, entailed the slaughter of dozens of sheep and cattle. A festival procession would be followed by the sacrifice, after which the meat would be prepared for a ritual feast. The cooked meat was divided into portions of equal size but variable quality; its distribution among the assembled worshipers was sometimes decided by lot, sometimes by the recipients' political and social status.

BELOW: **A small-scale procession toward an altar is depicted on this unusual wooden plaque, dated to ca. 530 BCE, from Pitsa, near Corinth. At the head of the procession a woman carries a tray of offerings and a jug. Behind her, a boy leads the sacrificial sheep, followed by musicians and branch-bearers.**

THE BEAUTIFUL CROWN OF ZEUS

BELOW: Epidauros was among the sanctuaries that hosted athletic events. Pictured here is the stadium, built in the 5th century BCE in a natural declivity, with seats partly carved out of the rock and partly built up. Both starting and finishing lines for the running race survive, around 590 feet (180 m) apart.

Some festivals held at local village or city level included athletic competitions, but the best known are the Panhellenic Games at the great interstate sanctuaries. These may have originated in the funeral games held in honor of the dead, such as those for Patroklos described in the *Iliad*, but they developed over time to include more and more events, with subdivisions for different age groups. The oldest were the games in honor of Zeus at Olympia, traditionally founded in 776 BCE, followed by the Pythian Games for Apollo at Delphi founded in 586 BCE, the Isthmian Games for Poseidon in 580 BCE, and the Nemean Games for Zeus in 573 BCE. The Olympic and Pythian Games were held once every four years, the Isthmian and Nemean

every two, and between them they made up a "circuit" (*periodos*). Special honors were accorded to "circuit-winners" (*periodonikos*)—individuals who had won victories at all four games. The prizes for the Panhellenic Games had no inherent value. Instead the victor in each event was awarded an honorific crown (*stephanos*), made of a plant that had a mythological connection with the sanctuary in question—wild olive at Olympia, laurel at Delphi, pine at the Isthmos, and wild celery at Nemea.

A special feature of the games at Olympia was the Olympic Truce, the terms of which stipulated that all states had to suspend any hostilities for several weeks either side of the festival to allow athletes safe passage to and from the games. The Olympic officials had the power to impose hefty fines on any state that broke the truce and ban its athletes from competing. The earliest games consisted only of the *stadion*, which was a sprint over a distance of a *stade*, or 600 feet (about 180 m), but longer footraces were added over time, the two-*stade diaulos*, the long-distance *dolichos* (ca. 16,000 feet, or nearly 5,000 m), and the grueling *hoplites*, run over a distance of 2 to 4 *stades* in full hoplite armor weighing around 56 lbs (25 kg). There was also wrestling, boxing and the *pankration* (a kind of all-in wrestling), and the *pentathlon*, which consisted of running, jumping, throwing the javelin and discus, and wrestling; two- and four-horse chariot racing and horse racing were accommodated in the hippodrome. By 400 BCE the games lasted for five days, instead of the original one. All males who were native Greek-speakers and free citizens were entitled to take part in the games, provided they were not ritually impure. Women were not usually allowed among the spectators, although exceptions were made for certain priestesses and virgins, and there was nothing to prevent women from entering teams in the chariot race, a competition in which the fourth-century BCE Spartan princess Kyniska won several victories.

BELOW: The young female competitors in Hera's games at Olympia (see page 57) had a mythological role model in the athletic Atalanta, depicted here in a 3rd- or 2nd-century BCE statuette. Unwilling to marry, Atalanta made suitors compete against her in a running race, which they would inevitably lose, until Hippomenes (or Melanion) finally got the better of her, with the help of some golden apples supplied by Aphrodite.

THE HUMAN FORM

Exercise and athletic competitions were common subjects in vase-painting, with runners (above) and boxers (left and right) both popular subjects. Sculptures were also commissioned in commemoration of notable victories, which provided the sculptor with an opportunity to display his mastery of the male nude. Pictured opposite is the "Victorious Youth," a rare bronze original of ca. 320–300 BCE found in 1961 in the Adriatic Sea north of Ancona, where it must have been shipwrecked on its way to Italy to be added to a Roman art collection. The young man stands in a relaxed pose, but the athlete's taut muscles are clearly delineated, and the right hand raised to his head draws attention to his victor's wreath.

SACRED MYSTERIES

Much of Greek religion placed an emphasis on the public performance of ritual rather than personal devotion, but a major exception can be seen in the mystery cults. The defining feature of a mystery cult was its element of secrecy, with access only granted to those who had undergone initiation. The rituals of most mystery cults remain obscure, but we have a certain amount of information about the myths that lay behind them and places where they were performed.

The best documented are the Mysteries of Demeter and Persephone at Eleusis, which flourished from at least the eighth century BCE to the sanctuary's destruction ca. 400 CE, and attracted initiates not just from Attica but from all over the Greek-speaking world. The location of the sanctuary is explained by the myth that Demeter found a welcome there during her search for her abducted daughter (see pages

RIGHT: **On this Attic red-figure *dinos* (wine-mixing bowl), dated ca. 470 BCE, the prince Triptolemos is depicted seated in Demeter's dragon-pulled chariot, holding the ears of wheat that he will bear all over the world. The goddess and her daughter Persephone stand to either side, one holding yet more wheat, the other holding a jug and *phiale* for making the libations that were customary at the start of a journey.**

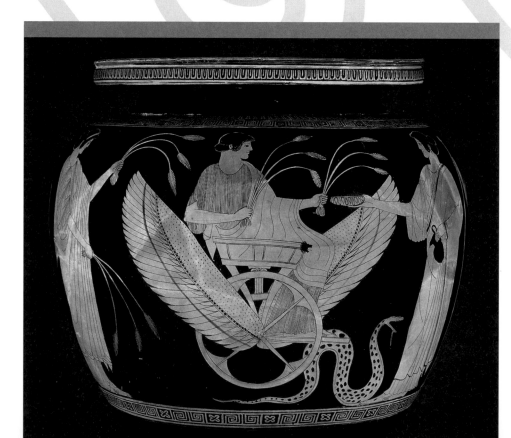

RIGHT: **This marble statue of ca. 340 BCE comes from the sanctuary of Demeter at Knidos and depicts the goddess at slightly larger than human scale, seated on a throne. She is heavily draped and modestly veiled. The statue's head was made separately, from better-quality Parian marble.**

60–61), as a reward for which she instructed the Eleusinians in her rites. On Persephone's safe return from Hades, Demeter restored fertility to the Earth and gave the Eleusinian prince Triptolemos the task of teaching agriculture to the rest of humankind. The Great Mysteries were celebrated every August in a week-long festival that included special purificatory rituals for the initiates and a grand procession from Athens along all 19 miles (30 km) of the Sacred Way to Eleusis. We do not know exactly what happened during the all-night initiation ceremony, but it seems to have involved drinking a special concoction, handling sacred objects, and watching some kind of performance dramatically lit by torches, possibly enacting the birth of a sacred child.

Also of wide repute were the Mysteries of the Great Gods celebrated on the island of Samothrace, in which Herodotus was an initiate. The sanctuary was especially built up in the fourth and third centuries BCE, its best known dedication being the Louvre's "Victory of Samothrace." The Samothracian Mysteries were supposed to offer protection from danger, but they may also have had an ethical element, since the initiate was asked to confess the worst deed he had ever committed. Hopes for the afterlife were also offered by the Bacchic mysteries of Dionysos (see pages 132–3), although these were not confined to performance in the context of a sanctuary.

PROPHETS AND ORACLES

In a world where every aspect of life was governed by the gods, it was clearly important to ascertain their will. This was especially vital when undertaking any hazardous enterprise, such as going on a journey, establishing a colony, or marching into battle, and many types of divination were practiced. At the most humble level an individual or family might cast lots or look for meaning in dreams, or in signs, which could be anything even slightly out of the ordinary, from a sudden sneeze to a chance encounter. The interpretation of more complex signs was the realm of professional seers, who might, for example, observe the flight of birds in search of good or bad omens. The entrails of sacrificial victims were also regularly consulted,

LEFT: Visitors to Apollo's oracle at Delphi had to purify themselves at the Kastalian Spring before entering the sanctuary proper. The spring was incorporated into an architectural structure ca. 600 BCE, but what can be seen today are the remains of a new structure set into the rocky side of the ravine in the 1st century BCE. The niches in the back wall would have held votive offerings.

the inspection of the liver being the special province of the haruspex; unless the liver was of the correct color and formation the undertaking was proclaimed to be doomed.

On particularly momentous occasions, both individuals and states would take their queries to sanctuaries that specialized in divination: the oracles. Apollo was especially associated with this prophetic power (see pages 72–3), but there were also several oracles of Zeus, and others with chthonic connections, such as the oracle of the hero Trophonios at Lebadeia, and of the Dead at Ephyra. The great sanctuary of Zeus Naios at Dodona claimed to be the oldest oracle in Greece, and, while it was occasionally consulted by cities, inscribed lead tablets from the site record many more personal enquiries: "Lysanias asks Zeus Naios and Dione whether the child with which Annyla is pregnant is not by him."

ABOVE: This Attic black-figure amphora of ca. 520 BCE depicts divination by haruspicy. A white-haired old man, who may be a priest or seer, gesticulates while a boy holds out an animal's liver for the soldier's inspection.

Most famous and authoritative of all were the oracles pronounced at Delphi by Apollo's mouthpiece, the priestess known as the Pythia. Recent geological investigations at Delphi suggest that she may have been put into a trance-like state by inhaling ethylene rising through fissures in the rocks below the temple, but her words were in any case often "translated" into verse by attendant priests. Herodotus is a particularly prolific, if not necessarily reliable, source for these verse oracles, which are characterized by their ambiguity and often result in a story with an ironic twist, as in the case of the Lydian king Croesus: on enquiring whether he should fight against Persia, he was told that if he did so he would destroy a mighty empire. Encouraged, Croesus went ahead with his campaign—and his own great empire was duly wiped out.

DELPHI: CENTER OF THE COSMOS

Despite its remote location on the slopes of Mount Parnassos, according to tradition Delphi lay at the very center of the world. Zeus once ascertained this by loosing two eagles at the outermost points of the universe, marking the place where they met with the *omphalos*—a curiously carved stone representing the Earth's "navel," a version of which was kept in the inner sanctum of Apollo's temple at Delphi. The *Homeric Hymn to Apollo* tells how Apollo at first chose a site by the spring Telphousa, but was persuaded by its eponymous nymph to settle higher up at Krisa. Here he determined to establish his oracle, and laid the foundations for his own temple, once he had dispatched a monstrous serpent, which he left to rot (*putho*); hence Delphi's alternative name "Pytho" and the "Pythian Games" held there.

Historically, Apollo's sanctuary seems to have been established in the tenth century BCE, with the oracle in operation by the eighth and the games added in the early sixth century BCE. Here we see the lower part of the sanctuary, popularly known as Marmaria ("the marbles"), which was sacred to Athene Pronaia ("Guardian of the Temple") or Pronoia ("Forethought"). Athene had a temple here from the seventh century BCE, and there are remains of two treasuries, one of which was dedicated in the late sixth century BCE by the people of Massilia (see pages 38–9). Although the early fourth-century Tholos ("Rotunda"), with three of its 20 Doric columns restored, is one of the most famous sights in Greece, we do not know what it was used for.

MASKS OF DIONYSOS

BELOW: From the 330s BCE onward the Theater of Dionysos at Athens had a marble auditorium that could seat 16,000–17,000 spectators. The front row, a section of which is shown here, consists of "thrones," each reserved for a priest or magistrate. The most elaborate throne at the center was reserved for the priest of Dionysos Eleuthereus himself.

According to Plutarch, the four winter months at Delphi were sacred to Dionysos, and a private group of women from Delphi, the Thyiades, worshiped Dionysos on the slopes of Parnassos with ecstatic nocturnal rituals. Admittance to a group (*thiasos*) of bacchants or maenads—women who "raved" (*mainomai*) for the god beyond the confines of the city—involved initiation that, like initiation into the Eleusinian Mysteries (see pages 126–7), might offer hopes for a blessed life after death. There are a number of vase-paintings showing the women who worship Dionysos wearing the maenads' animal skins and ivy crowns, and carrying the *thyrsos*, torches, and drums, but also engaging in the quite normal cult activities of drinking wine and dancing.

The more public side to Dionysos' worship can be seen in festivals such as the Anthesteria, which celebrated his association with wine, or those that included dramatic contests. At Athens one of these was the Lenaia, an internal city affair from which foreigners and metics were excluded, celebrated for three days in January, with a procession and performances of both tragedies and comedies. On a larger scale, and well attended by non-Athenians, was the City Dionysia, which coincided with the opening of the sailing season in early March. The festival lasted for five days, beginning with processions to the temple of Dionysos Eleuthereus beside the Theater of Dionysos on the south slope of the Akropolis. A great feast was followed by the *komos*, a very informal procession in which men ran through the streets singing and dancing, and the dramatic contests began early the next morning. Three tragic playwrights each

presented a trilogy, such as Aeschylus' *Oresteia* (see pages 108–109), followed by a satyr-play, a light-hearted rendering of a familiar mythological story featuring a chorus of satyrs. Five comic playwrights each competed with a single play, and each of the ten tribes (see pages 28–9) entered choruses for the men's and the boys' competitions in the *dithyramb*, Dionysos' special hymn.

ABOVE: This detail of the late 2nd-century BCE marble "Borghese Krater" shows a maenad dancing with a drum; the young Dionysos stands to her left.

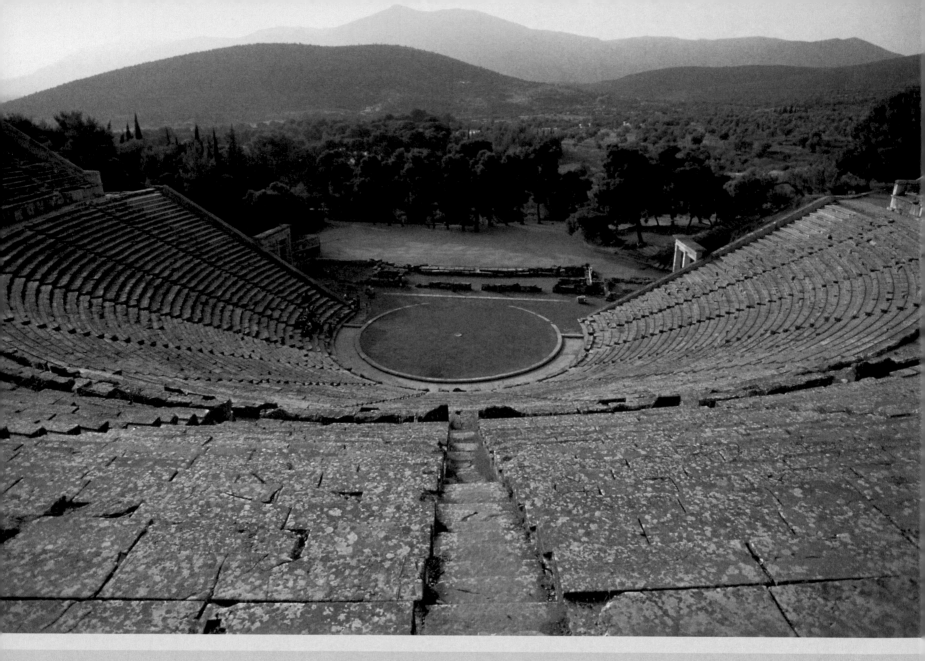

THE THEATER OF EPIDAUROS

Asklepios, god of healing, was often encountered at an individual level. Like Herakles, Asklepios was originally a hero, son of Apollo and a mortal woman Koronis. Asklepios learned the arts of medicine from the Centaur Cheiron and spent his adult life healing the sick. He was eventually struck down by Zeus' thunderbolt for having presumptuously tried to raise a man from the dead, but despite his death, which should have limited him to heroic cult, Asklepios was paid divine honors from at least 500 BCE. From the late fifth century CE his cult spread throughout the Greek world, with notable sanctuaries on Kos and at Pergamon, and was even exported to Rome in 293 BCE.

The most important center of Asklepios' worship, however, was the sanctuary at Epidauros in the Argolid, which attracted visitors from all over Greece and beyond, who left inscribed records of their miraculous cures. This private invocation of Asklepios by the sick in their hour of need was counterbalanced by the worship of whole communities at regular festivals, such as the Athenian Asklepieia and Epidauria. At Epidauros, the annual festival included athletic events, catered for by a wrestling ground and stadium whose remains can still be visited (see illustration, page 122), and dramatic competitions held in the spectacular theater, shown here. This was constructed in the mid-fourth century BCE, when the whole sanctuary underwent extensive monumentalization, making use of the natural slope of the hill to support 55 rows of seating, for 13,000–14,000 spectators. The theater was found in near perfect condition when it was excavated in the late nineteenth century CE. Today it is used for an annual summer festival of classical drama.

GLOSSARY

agora "Market-place"—used today especially of the Athenian Agora, but every city had one.

akropolis The "upper city" or "citadel"—the term is specially associated with the Athenian Akropolis.

amphora Narrow-necked vessel for storing and transporting wine or oil; some types have a pair of handles on the neck or belly. In the eighth century BCE outsize amphoras were also used as grave-markers.

archaic Applied to the period ca.750–500 BCE, sometimes thought of as beginning in 776 BCE, the traditional foundation date of the Olympic Games, and often extended to include the Persian Wars (490–79 BCE). A certain formality and stylization is associated with art of the period.

classical Properly speaking, the classical period consists of the fifth and fourth centuries BCE, and is often defined as the era from the end of the Persian Wars (479 BCE) to the death of Alexander (323 BCE).

frieze On a temple or treasury, the frieze usually runs along the top of the columns around the building's exterior. In the Doric architectural order the frieze consists of metopes (see below) interspersed with triglyphs (blocks carved with a | | | pattern), while the Ionic frieze is a continuous strip usually decorated with relief sculpture. The term "frieze" is also used to indicate a strip of decoration on a painted vase.

geometric Term applied to pottery of the ninth and eighth centuries BCE because of the geometric patterning of its decoration; also used of the period ca.900–700 BCE. "Protogeometric" is used for the pottery of the preceding two centuries.

Hellene From *hellên*, the word used by the Greeks to refer to themselves, with *Hellas* denoting the collection of city-states making up the territory of "Greece."

Hellenistic The period from the death of Alexander (323 BCE) to the Battle of Actium (31 BCE). Earlier end-dates sometimes used are 86 BCE (fall of Athens to the Romans) or 146 BCE (sack of Corinth by the Romans).

hoplite A heavily armed infantryman—from *hoplon*, a type of large shield.

hydria Narrow-necked vessel for fetching and serving water, with a pair of horizontal handles either side of the belly (for lifting) and a third vertical handle on the neck (for pouring).

kore Literally "maiden," used to describe a free-standing female sculpture of the archaic period.

kouros Literally "youth," used to describe a free-standing male sculpture of the archaic period.

krater Bowl for mixing wine and water (Greeks generally drank 2 parts wine to 5 of water). A variety of types are further qualified by the shape of their body (bell krater) or handles (calyx and volute kraters).

lekythos Small vessel with long narrow neck for valuable liquids like perfumed oil. "White-ground" lekythoi were especially used as grave-goods.

metope More or less square slab in a Doric frieze (see above), often decorated with relief sculpture.

pediment The triangular space formed by the gable-ends of a temple or treasury, often decorated with figures sculpted in relief or in the round.

polis "City-state" (pl. *poleis*): encompasses the physical city, its people, government, and public affairs.

stele (pl. *stelai*) Marble slab, with relief sculpture and/or an inscription, often erected in memory of the dead (funerary *stele*) or in honor of a god (votive *stele*), or to record a public decree.

FOR MORE INFORMATION

American School of Classical Studies at Athens
54 Souidias Street
GR-106 76 Athens
Greece
In the United States:
6-8 Charlton Street
Princeton, NJ 08540-5232
(609) 683-0800
Web site: http://www.ascsa.edu.gr
This organization provides graduate students and scholars from affilliated North American colleges and universities with a base in Greece for the advanced study of Greek culture—from antiquity to today.

The Ancient Greek World
University of Pennsylvania Museum of Archaeology and Anthropology
3260 South Street
Philadelphia, PA 19104
(215) 898-4000
Web site: http://www.museum.upenn.edu/Greek_World/index.html
This Web site offers descriptions of the land, culture, daily life, religion, and economy of the ancient Greek world.

Department of Greek and Roman Studies
University of Victoria
P.O. Box 3045
Victoria, BC V8W 3P4
Canada
(250) 721-8514
Web site: http://web.uvic.ca/grs/department_files/classical_myth/index.html

The Web site Classical Myth: The Ancient Sources, which is maintained by the university's Department of Greek and Roman Studies, features images and texts about the Olympian gods and a timeline of Greek history and literature.

History for Kids
Portland State University
Portland, OR 97207
Web site: http://www.historyforkids.org
Kidipede, or history for kids, provides information about human history, including Ancient Greece and mythology.

Metropolitan Museum of Art
Department of Greek and Roman Art
1000 Fifth Avenue
New York, NY 10028-0198
(212) 535-7710
Web site: http://www.metmuseum.org/Works_of_Art/greek_and_roman_art
The collection of Greek and Roman art at the Metropolitan Museum of Art, more than 17,000 works ranging in date from the Neolithic period to the time of the Roman emperor Constantine's conversion to Christianity in 312 CE, includes the art of many cultures and is among the most comprehensive in North America.

National Junior Classical League
422 Wells Mill Drive
Miami University
Oxford, OH 45056-1694
(513) 529-7741

Web site: http://www.njcl.org
This organization of junior and senior high school students is sponsored by the American Classical League. It encourages an interest in and appreciation of the language, art, literature, and culture of ancient Greece and Rome.

The Perseus Digital Library
Tufts University
Medford, MA 02155
Web site: http://www.perseus.tufts.edu
This digital library provides information on the humanities and offers collections on history, literature, and culture of the Greco-Roman world.

WEB SITES

Due to the changing nature of Internet links, Rosen Publishing has developed an online list of Web sites related to the subject of this book. This site is updated regularly. Please use this link to access this list:

http://www.rosenlinks.com/civ/gree

FOR FURTHER READING

Barringer, J. M. *Art, Myth, and Ritual in Classical Greece*. Cambridge, England: Cambridge University Press, 2008.

Beard, M. *The Parthenon*. London, England: Profile Books, 2002.

Brulé, P. *Women of Ancient Greece*. (Translated by Antonia Nevill.) Edinburgh, Scotland: Edinburgh University Press, 2003.

Bugh, G. R., ed. *The Cambridge Companion to the Hellenistic World*. Cambridge, England: Cambridge University Press, 2006.

Erskine, A., ed. *A Companion to the Hellenistic World*. Oxford, England: Blackwell, 2005.

Hall, J. M. *A History of the Archaic Greek World ca. 1200-479 BC*. Oxford, England: Oxford University Press, 2007.

Hornblower, S. *The Greek World 479–323 BC*. 3rd ed. London, England, and New York, NY: Routledge, 2002.

Kinzl, K. H., ed. *A Companion to the Classical Greek World*. Oxford, England: Oxford University Press, 2006.

Lapatin, K. *Mysteries of the Snake Goddess: Art, Desire and the Forging of History*. Boston, MA, and New York, NY: Houghton Mifflin Company, 2002.

Larson, J. *Ancient Greek Cults: A Guide*. London, England, and New York, NY: Routledge, 2007.

Lewis, S. *The Athenian Woman: an Iconographic Handbook*. London, England, and New York, NY: Routledge, 2002.

McKeown, N. *The Invention of Ancient Slavery*. London, England: Duckworth, 2002.

Mikalson, J. *Ancient Greek Religion*. Oxford, England: Blackwell, 2004.

Moignard, E. *Greek Vases: An Introduction*. London, England: Duckworth, 2006.

Morales, H. *Classical Myth: A Very Short Introduction*. Oxford, England: Oxford University Press, 2007.

Morris, I., and B. B. Powell. *The Greeks: History, Culture, and Society*. Upper Saddle River, NJ: Pearson Prentice Hall, 2005.

Ogden, D., ed. *A Companion to Greek Religion*. Oxford, England: Blackwell, 2007.

Osborne, R. *Archaic and Classical Greek Art*. Oxford, England, and New York, NY: Oxford University Press, 1998.

Osborne, R. *Athens and Athenian Democracy*. Cambridge, England: Cambridge University Press, 2010.

Osborne, R. *Greece in the Making 1200–479 BC*. 2nd ed. London, England, and New York, NY: Routledge, 2008.

Osborne, R. *Greek History*. London, England, and New York, NY: Routledge, 2004.

Pedley, J. G. *Sanctuaries and the Sacred in the Ancient Greek World*. Cambridge, England: Cambridge University Press, 2005.

Pomeroy, S. B., S. M. Burstein, W. Donlan, and J. T. Roberts. *A Brief History of Ancient Greece*. Oxford, England: Oxford University Press, 2004.

Raaflaub, K. A., and H. van Wees, eds. *A Companion to Archaic Greece*. Oxford, England: Wiley-Blackwell, 2007.

Samons, L. J., II ed. *The Cambridge Companion to the Age of Pericles*. Cambridge, England: Cambridge University Press, 2007.

Shapiro, H. A. ed. *The Cambridge Companion to Archaic Greece*. Cambridge, England: Cambridge University Press, 2007.

Spivey, N. *The Ancient Olympics*. Oxford, England: Oxford University Press, 2004.

Stewart, A. *Classical Art and the Birth of Western Art*. Cambridge, England: Cambridge University Press, 2008.

Valavanis, P. *Games and Sanctuaries in Ancient Greece*. Los Angeles, CA: J. P. Getty Museum, 2004.

Woodford, S. *Images of Myths in Classical Antiquity*. Cambridge, England: Cambridge University Press, 2003.

INDEX

ABOUT THE AUTHOR

Dr. Emma J. Stafford lectures on Greek cultural history, especially on religion, myth, and art, at the University of Leeds in the United Kingdom. She is author of *Worshipping Virtues: Personification and the Divine in Ancient Greece.*

PICTURE CREDITS

The publisher would like to thank the following people, museums, and photographic libraries for permission to reproduce their material. Every care has been taken to trace copyright holders. However, if we have omitted anyone we apologize and will, if informed, make corrections to any future edition.

Key:
AA = The Art Archive, London
AKG = A.K.G., London
Ashmolean = Ashmolean Museum, Oxford
BAL = Bridgeman Art Library, London
Getty Museum = Getty Museum, Malibu, California
Scala = Scala, Florence

Page 1 Getty Museum; **3** Getty Museum; **6** Scala; **7** Getty Museum; **8** British Museum, London; **9** Axiom, London/James Morris; **10–11** BAL; **12** Getty Museum; **14** Louvre, Paris/BAL; **15** Museo Archeologico Nazionale, Naples/BAL; **16–17** BAL; **18** Getty Museum; **19** Louvre, Paris/BAL; **20** Ashmolean/BAL; **21** Paestum/AKG/Erich Lessing; **22** National Archaeological Museum, Athens/BAL; **24** Axiom, London/Luke White; **25** Private Collection/AKG; **26** Villa Giulia Rome/AKG; **27** BAL; **28** Agora Museum, Athens/AKG; **29** Wadsworth Atheneum, Hartford, Connecticut/Gift of J. Pierpont Morgan; **30** Ashmolean/BAL; **33** British Museum, London/BAL; **34** British Museum, London/BAL; **35** Louvre, Paris/BAL; **36** British Museum, London/BAL; **37** National Museum of Scotland/BAL; **38** Museo Capitolini, Rome/AKG; **39** Musée Archeologique, Châtillon-sur-Seine/BAL; **40–41** Scala; **42** Louvre, Paris/BAL; **43** AA; **44** British Museum, London/Michael Holford, Essex; **45** Getty Museum; **46–47** Louvre, Paris/BAL; **47** Ashmolean/BAL; **48** Louvre, Paris/BAL; **49** Louvre, Paris/BAL; **51** Archaelogical Museum, Delphi/BAL; **52–53** The AA/Dagli Orti; **54** Louvre, Paris/BAL; **55** Antikenmuseum, Berlin/AKG/Erich Lessing; **56** British Museum, London/Michael Holford, Essex; **57** AA; **58** National Archaeological Museum, Athens/BAL; **59** BAL/John Bethell; **60** Ashmolean/BAL; **61** Staatliche Antikensamlungen, Munich/AKG/Erich Lessing; **62** Archaeological Museum, Corinth/AA; **64** Ashmolean/BAL; **65** Axiom, London/Doug Mc Kinlay; **66** Louvre, Paris/BAL; **67 above** British Museum, London/Michael Holford, Essex; **67 below** Getty Museum; **68** Louvre, Paris/BAL; **69** British Museum, London/ Michael Holford, Essex; **70–71** Corbis, London; **72** Louvre, Paris/BAL; **73** Vatican Museums and Galleries/Scala; **74** British Museum, London/Michael Holford, Essex; **75** Archaeological Museum, Piraeus/AA; **76–77** Corbis, London; **78** Louvre, Paris/BAL; **79** Staatliche Antikensamlungen, Munich/ AKG/Erich Lessing; **80** Louvre, Paris/BAL; **81** Getty Museum; **83** Louvre, Paris/BAL; **84** Museo Nazionale, Reggio Calabria/AKG; **85** Louvre, Paris/BAL; **86** Sparta Museum/AKG; **87** Private Collection/Werner Forman Archive; **89** Mykonos Museum/AKG; **90** Ashmolean Museum/BAL; **91** British Museum, London/BAL; **92–93** Corbis, London; **94** Olympia Museum/AKG; **95** Museo Nazionale, Naples/Scala; **97** Louvre, Paris/BAL; **98** Heraklion Archaeological Museum/AKG; **100** Vatican Museums and Galleries/BAL; **101** Museo Archeologico, Bari/BAL; **102** Getty Museum; **103** Louvre, Paris/BAL; **104** Birmingham Museum and Art Gallery/BAL; **105** Hermitage, St. Petersburg/BAL; **106** Vatican Museums and Galleries/Scala; **107** Getty Museum; **108** Louvre, Paris/BAL; **109** Museo Archaeologico Nazionale, Naples/BAL; **110** University of Tübingen; **111** British Museum, London/BAL; **112** Musée Condé, Chantilly/BAL; **113** British Museum, London; **114** Getty Museum; **115** Archaeological Museum, Piraeus/AA/Dagli Onti; **116** Getty Museum; **117** BAL; **119** Corbis, London; **120** British Museum, London/Michael Holford, Essex; **121** National Archaeological Museum, Athens/Scala; **122** Emma Stafford; **123** Louvre, Paris/BAL; **124** Getty Museum; **126** Getty Museum; **127** British Museum, London/BAL; **128** Werner Forman Archive; **129** Château-Musée, Bologne-sur-Mer/AKG; **130–131** Michael Holford, Essex; **132** BAL; **133** Louvre, Paris/BAL; **133–134** Corbis, London.